OBAMA:
Our
National
Nightmare

FOR GOD AND COUNTRY

OBAMA

Our National Nightmare

Nelson Anderson

"WHEN I WAS A BOY, I WAS TOLD THAT ANYBODY COULD BECOME PRESIDENT. NOW, I'M BEGINNING TO BELIEVE IT."

Clarence Darrow
(1857-1938)

CHAPTER 1

HIS BACKGROUND WAS UNKNOWN. He didn't share the values of his countrymen. He had no experience in national security, foreign policy, business, or economics. His singular qualification for the presidency was an exceptional talent for speaking. Yet here he stood, the most powerful man on earth, preparing to give his inaugural address before nearly two million adoring fans.

Facing freezing temperatures, a transportation system that ground to a halt, and a persons-to-bathroom ratio of approximately ten-thousand-to-one, this unprecedented sea of humanity crammed the National Mall in Washington on January 20, 2009. Many spent their last dollar or quit their jobs to make the trip; being there was that important.

A mania had swept the country—and especially the media—since Barack Obama burst onto the national stage just four years earlier. The adulation prompted his wife to quip, "Someday, maybe he'll deserve all the attention."

How had this bit player in the Chicago political machine risen so far, so fast, and with so little scrutiny? Answer: Barack Obama is a salesman *par excellence*.

Nothing in Obama's life ever prepared him for the responsibilities of the presidency, even under the best of circumstances. To use an analogy any parent can appreciate, the American people took an inexperienced driver and put him into heavy traffic.

This community organizer, part-time college instructor, and junior senator wasn't prepared to become president this early—and in a rare moment of humility, he admitted as much. Shortly after his election to the Senate in 2004, Obama was asked if he planned to seek the White House four years hence. His response was classic Obama:

"I was elected yesterday. I have never set foot in the U.S. Senate. I've never worked in Washington. And the notion that somehow I'm immediately going to start running for higher office just doesn't make sense…So look, I can unequivocally say I will not be running for national office in four years."

He started running immediately, of course. Senator Hillary Rodham Clinton was universally regarded as the Democratic front-runner, so the young politico had little to lose. Obama was running to burnish his credentials, expand his name identification, and establish himself as the Democrats' putative front-runner next time around. It was a practice run for a real campaign in 2012, 2016, or beyond, by which point he might have some actual accomplishments under his belt.

Except that he ended up winning. Owing to once-in-a-lifetime circumstances, Barack Obama, the man from nowhere, was elected the forty-fourth president of the United States.

It is said that all of life is a lesson, if only you'll allow it to be. In 2008, angry voters wanted to send a message to Washington. What they *didn't* bargain for was a sweeping expansion of government that puts Washington in charge of every aspect of their lives. This is the law of unintended consequences.

Fool me once, shame on you. Fool me twice…

IT IS RARE FOR ONE political party to hold the White House for more than two consecutive terms. Since World War II, that's happened only once, when the elder President Bush rode Ronald Reagan's coattails into office to cinch twelve years of Republican control. Thus, after two terms of George W. Bush, the Democrats could have nominated George Costanza in 2008 and still won the presidency.

By late that summer, however, the voters weren't buying Obama's shtick. Republican nominee John McCain held a lead in the Gallup Poll for nine consecutive days in mid-September, putting Obama's coronation into serious jeopardy. Democrats fretted that they'd nominated the one candidate capable of losing in the most anti-Republican cycle in four decades.

But the implosion of Lehman Brothers—the nation's largest bankruptcy—on September 15 triggered an international financial crisis just seven weeks before the election. With the economy on the brink of collapse, the incumbent Republicans were suddenly *personae non gratae*. The financial meltdown could not have been timed more perfectly for Obama. From that date forward, McCain never held the lead again.

The sad part is that McCain had nothing to do with the crisis. In fact, it was McCain who sounded the alarm years earlier about the excesses of the housing market, especially with regard to mortgage giants Fannie Mae and Freddie Mac. The veteran senator crusaded against out-of-control borrowing and spending his entire career, often as a lone voice in the wilderness, and yet *he* was ultimately punished for the ensuing financial meltdown.

A case could be made that the Democrats' housing and banking policies, dating to the Community Reinvestment Act of 1977, which forced lenders to make loans in low-income neighborhoods under the guise of "fairness," were largely responsible for the collapse of 2008. Irony doesn't get much thicker.

No one ever said representative democracy is perfect; restless voters are often driven more by emotion than by logic. As the nominee of the out-of-power party, Obama was the beneficiary of voter angst and anger. Had the crisis struck two months later, he'd still be the freshman senator from Illinois.

Sir Winston Churchill put it best: "Democracy is the worst form of government—with the exception of all the others."

On November 4, 2008, the longest presidential campaign in history, featuring media saturation of Obama for two interminable years, was over. Election night found the national press fawning over its own creation: President-elect Barack Hussein Obama.

That the Democrat was held to under 53 percent of the vote is remarkable, given the circumstances, but that didn't stop the media from portraying his victory as a landslide of Reaganesque proportions. Euphoric reporters could hardly contain their emotion. This man, we were told, is postracial, postpartisan, nonideological, and ready to bring this sorely divided nation together.

We've learned the hard way that the narrative was wrong. The charade was over, and off came the mask.

OBAMA WASN'T ONLY LUCKY; he was idolized by the media. Probing, inquiring, unbiased reporting is *de rigueur* for a healthy representative democracy, but in 2008, objective journalism was as dead as the subprime mortgage market. Democratic operative Terry McAuliffe acknowledged that 90 percent of the media were in the tank for Obama. All hard-hitting questions and investigations were deemed to be off limits.

Only Fox News, talk radio, the Drudge Report, and the conservative blogosphere unearthed Obama's background, associations, voting record, and lack of executive experience. The rest of the national media gave him a pass. As one commentator remarked, classroom teachers are vetted more scrupulously.

"It's almost hard to remain objective, because he's so infectious!" gushed Lee Cowan of NBC News.

Media personnel are overwhelmingly left of center by their nature; as in the entertainment and academic worlds, the gravitational pull of journalism draws liberal personalities to its ranks. Candidate Obama represented everything that attracted idealistic young reporters to the profession: he was hip, cool, liberal—and black. This was no ordinary campaign; this was a once-in-a-millennium opportunity to make history. Journalists felt an obligation to advocate for his candidacy, lest the moment pass them by. In their minds, this moral imperative eclipsed industry standards of ethics and impartiality.

The third pillar of Obama's meteoric rise was his dazzling speeches—his principal claim to fame before ascending to the presidency.

I attended an Obama rally in Las Vegas during the closing days of the campaign. *Why*, I'm still not certain. It might have been out of morbid curiosity, or perhaps I just wanted to make sense of all the hysteria surrounding this otherwise unaccomplished politician.

The pandemonium was at the same time mystifying and disturbing. The atmosphere was truly cultlike. Stories of fainting spells at Obama speeches were legendary. My seven-year-old nephew and niece have never been this delirious, even on Christmas morning.

I sat beside a young woman who was especially star-struck. We made small talk before the event, and I learned that she and her friends were students at the University of Nevada, Las Vegas. When Obama finished his speech (none too soon for me), my seatmates were bursting with excitement: "He's so inspiring, the way he just speaks from the heart!"

Call me a fuddy-duddy, but I wasn't feeling it. These students were young and naïve—barely drinking age, if that—and they'd probably never followed politics before. There's plenty of time for this video-game generation to grow up and experience the real world. Or so I could pray.

Give the man his due: Obama delivers his speeches with a panache rarely seen among celebrities, much less politicians. Who knows; were I an idealistic college kid again, I just might have fallen victim, too.

OBAMA'S SPEECHES ARE SOARING and his rhetoric inspiring, provided those trusty teleprompters are at the ready. Without them, the man is lost.

That's putting it mildly. At a campaign rally in Bristol, Virginia, Obama faced his worst nightmare: his teleprompters abruptly malfunctioned in the middle of his speech. The candidate was forced to ad-lib, and the results weren't pretty:

"If you send a kid to the emergency room for a treatable illness like asthma, they end up taking up a hospital bed, it costs [teleprompter stops working] when, if you, they just gave, you gave treatment early, and they got some treatment, and, uh, uh, a breathalyzer—or, an inhalator, not a breathalyzer [laughter]. I haven't had much sleep in the last forty-eight hours.

"What they'll say is, well it costs too much money, but, you know what, it would cost, it, it, it would cost about the same as what we would spend in, oh, over the course of ten years it would cost what it would cost us if, uh, heh heh, all right, okay, we're going to. The, it would cost us about the same as it would cost...for, about...hold on one second. I can't hear myself. Ah, but I'm glad you're fired up though!"

And Bush was inarticulate?

TO WIN THE RIGHT to face McCain, Obama had to vanquish an even grittier opponent, former First Lady Hillary Clinton. This would require an enormous feat of political jujitsu; the Clintons defined politics as a blood sport. Strategist James Carville once quipped that if an opponent were drowning, he'd toss him an anchor. Nice people.

Still, when it came to getting down and dirty, the Clintons were no match for the Chicago political machine, the real power behind Obama's throne.

Clinton's game plan was to treat her young colleague deferentially, allowing his inexperience to speak for itself over the course of the primary campaign. But as it turned out, Obama's harshest critic wasn't Clinton at all; it was Senator Joe Biden of Delaware, another rival for the Democratic nomination. When asked if Obama was ready to be president, Biden was unequivocal: "I think he can be ready, but right now I don't believe he is. The presidency is not something that lends itself to on-the-job training."

Given a chance to clarify the remarks at a later debate, Biden tersely replied, "I stand by the statement."

Biden, of course, was later chosen as Obama's running mate. In politics, all can be forgiven in the name of ambition.

CHAPTER 2

EVEN OBAMA'S SUPPORTERS COULDN'T come up with a rationale for backing him. Prior to the Texas caucuses, Chris Matthews of MSNBC behaved like a real journalist for once, peppering Texas Senator Kirk Watson with tough questions about Obama's credentials:

Matthews: "You're a big Barack supporter, right, senator?"

Watson: "I am, yes, I am."

Matthews: "Well, name some of his legislative accomplishments."

Watson: "We, uh…"

Matthews: "No, senator, I want you to name some of Barack Obama's legislative accomplishments tonight, if you can."

[Several seconds of silence.]

Watson: "Well, I, you know, I, what I will talk about is more about what he's offering to the American people…"

Matthews: "No, no… You have to give me his accomplishments. You've supported him for president, you're on national television. Name his legislative accomplishments, sir."

[Several more seconds of silence.]

Watson: "Well, I, I'm not going to be able to name you specifics..."

Matthews: "Can you name any?"

Watson: "No, I'm not going to be able to do that..."

Matthews: "Well, that's a problem, isn't it?"

To Democrats, however, it wasn't a problem. For eight years, liberals marinated in their hatred for all things Bush. The 2008 election was, at long last, their chance for revenge. They scoured the political landscape for the proverbial anti-Bush, and this relative unknown with the "exotic" background and unusual name—not to mention universally favorable media coverage—fit the bill.

Clinton's campaign strategy backfired monumentally: Democratic voters couldn't have cared less about a candidate's experience, maturity, or qualifications. The miscalculation cost the New York senator her dream of becoming the nation's first female commander in chief.

As improbable as it seems, Obama ran to the *left* of Clinton in the primaries, particularly on the central issue of national security. So he needed a tour guide to find his way around Capitol Hill. Who cares? The political newcomer endeared himself to the lunatic fringe of the Democratic Party by promising to all but disassemble Bush's war on terror.

THE ENTERTAINMENT VALUE OF the Clinton-Obama slugfest was priceless. Bill Clinton came completely unglued, making little secret of his contempt for the brash neophyte. Ahead of the New Hampshire primary, the gravelly voiced former president established a new standard for sarcasm by mocking Obama in the first person:

"It doesn't matter that I started running for president less than a year after I got to the Senate...I am a great speaker, and a charismatic figure, and I'm the only one that had the judgment to oppose this war [Iraq] from the beginning—always, always, always...Give me a break. This whole thing is the biggest fairy tale I've ever seen."

The press, now a full-fledged apparatus of the Obama campaign, framed Clinton's "fairy tale" tantrum as a racist attack on Obama's historic candidacy. Beginning with the South Carolina primary, African-American voters hopped aboard the Obama bandwagon in record numbers. The Clintons were toast.

Throw out the old rulebook; the episode heralded a new era in presidential politics. Henceforth, any criticism of Obama, no matter how reasonable and relevant, would be deemed racist.

Another victim of the media's new rules of engagement was former vice presidential candidate Geraldine Ferraro. The first woman named to a major party ticket, and a liberal Democrat, no less, was flayed in the press for stating the obvious: "If Obama was a white man, he would not be in this position. And if he was a woman of any color, he would not be in this position. He happens to be very lucky to be who he is. And the country is caught up in the concept."

Ferraro was comparing her own historic candidacy with Obama's; she has acknowledged that she was chosen as Walter Mondale's running mate in 1984 over more qualified males. True to form, the media never portrayed her comments from that perspective.

Instead, she was called a racist.

The Obama camp angrily demanded an apology. To her credit, Ferraro held her ground: "Every time that campaign is upset about something, they call it racist." Thereafter, the onetime Democratic trailblazer was banished to political Siberia.

For months, prognosticators wrung their hands over the "Bradley effect," a theory which holds that white voters will lie to friends and pollsters about their intention to vote for a nonwhite candidate. Its name derives from the California gubernatorial campaign of 1982, in which Democrat Tom Bradley fared better in polls than he actually performed on Election Day. However, the Bradley effect, while a hot topic for political pundits, is junk science:

Bradley, then mayor of Los Angeles, held a modest lead in most pre-election surveys over his Republican rival, George Deukmejian. But shortly before Election Day, Bradley came out in support of a proposition which would have frozen the purchase of new handguns in California. The result was a larger-than-expected turnout by conservative voters, and a one-point win for Deukmejian.

Fast forward to 2008, and the possibility of a Bradley effect was a source of severe gastric distress for Obama's devoted media contingent. Liberal commentators slathered on the guilt, questioning whether this white-majority nation was ready to elect a black president.

Obviously, it was. But the pundits missed the point: the question was never about race. The voters' hesitation was always about Barack Obama himself.

If anything, Obama benefited from a "reverse" Bradley effect. Factoring in whites who were excited about (or shamed into) voting for the first serious African-American presidential candidate, along with the record black and ethnic-minority turnouts, Obama ultimately won more votes as a result of his race than he lost.

IT GALLED HILLARY THAT her former protégé—she had mentored Obama when he first arrived in Washington and even raised funds for him—continued to run one step ahead of her.

He couldn't hold a candle to her in debates. In her view, he was a featherweight contender; she was the heavyweight champ. His achievements were minimal, comically so; she claimed three decades of liberal activism. He burst onto the scene overnight; she'd spent years enduring insults, indignities, and vast, right-wing conspiracies (or so she believed). Now, her own people were abandoning her, and she couldn't understand it.

No fewer than four times, Hillary conferred an unofficial endorsement on McCain, the Republican nominee-in-waiting: "I have a lifetime of experience that I will bring to the White House. I know Senator McCain has a lifetime of experience that he will bring to the White House. And Senator Obama has a speech he gave in 2002."

Clinton's frustration was understandable; she actually garnered 176,000 more popular votes than Obama, once all states and territories were fairly counted. Obama, however, gamed the Democrats' byzantine nominating system to secure more delegates and eke out a victory. The mystery man would be the party's standard bearer going into the fall campaign. The Democrats, to use Bill Clinton's words, had rolled the dice.

The American people were anxious to scratch their eight-year itch and vote straight Democrat in 2008. What they *weren't* prepared for was an unknown quantity like Obama. In terms of readiness to serve as commander in chief, McCain was a man to Obama's child. How often in history have one candidate's credentials so dwarfed those of the other?

While Obama possessed no discernible qualifications to be president, McCain boasted a distinguished military career with an unparalleled record of service and bravery. The navy pilot spent over five years as a prisoner of war in Vietnam, enduring torture, malnutrition, and unspeakable conditions at the hands of the Vietcong, yet he refused to go home until every man captured before him was released as well.

The Arizona senator spent years engaging in foreign policy and was, in many respects, the Senate's go-to man on national-security matters. Despite his presidential heft, however, McCain's age surely cost him votes. At seventy-two, he would have been the oldest first-term president in American history.

A moderate Republican, McCain was at odds with his party's conservatives on issues ranging from immigration to campaign finance reform to interrogation of terror suspects. He bucked his party by opposing the Bush tax cuts and joining the "Gang of Fourteen," which effectively preserved the Senate filibuster for judicial nominations. At times, he appeared to relish his skirmishes with the Republican base more than with liberal Democrats. Rush Limbaugh and other conservatives branded McCain a RINO—"Republican in Name Only."

Ideologically speaking, the GOP selected a nominee who was clearly middle of the road. If only the Democrats could have said the same.

Poor polling and sluggish fundraising nearly forced McCain out of the Republican primary months earlier. Only through a fluky sequence of events did he chance upon the nomination. His conservative opponents, principally Mitt Romney, Mike Huckabee, and Fred Thompson, were busy canceling out each others' votes in early states. That afforded McCain a window of opportunity just wide enough through which to snatch the nomination.

McCain attempted to mend fences with the party's right wing in time for the fall campaign. Still, conservatives only grudgingly warmed to his candidacy. "It's like kissing your sister," grumbled one.

(After the election, Colin Powell castigated the GOP for allegedly ignoring its moderate wing. The Republicans had nominated the least conservative candidate in their field—one whose positions on many issues were indistinguishable from Obama's—and yet Powell chided the party for shunning its moderates. The media presented his grievances as gospel.)

IN ANY OTHER YEAR, MCCAIN would have steamrolled his upstart rival. But 2008 was no ordinary election season, and McCain's strengths in defense and foreign policy were largely off the table. It's striking that just seven years after 9/11, national security was no longer a pressing concern to the American electorate.

Former Representative Tom Davis of Virginia put it this way: "People were hungry for change, and [Obama] was running against a seventy-two-year-old guy who couldn't use a computer."

McCain liked to joke that he had to rely on his wife to use the Internet. That was consistent with his penchant for poking fun at himself, but it wasn't really true. As chairman of the Senate Commerce, Science, and Technology Committee throughout much of the Internet era, McCain was closely involved with information technology issues.

In fact, the senator suffered multiple injuries to his shoulders as a prisoner of war, making use of a keyboard painful. Routine tasks like raising his arms above his head were all but impossible. That didn't stop the Obama campaign from running ads mocking McCain for admitting "he still doesn't know how to use a computer" and "[he] can't send an e-mail."

The quirky McCain had established a maverick reputation when he was battling Bush for the Republican nomination eight years earlier. His off-the-cuff manner charmed reporters, who responded with overwhelmingly favorable coverage. But that was then. Running as the moderate alternative to Bush in 2000, McCain was a media darling. Running as the moderate alternative to Obama in 2008, he wasn't feeling the love. His media admirers, fickle bunch that they are, ran off with a newer, younger, more liberal suitor.

The *New York Times* launched the first salvo against the Republican nominee with an entirely unsubstantiated hit piece alleging a relationship between McCain and a female lobbyist. Meanwhile, the mainstream media ignored persistent rumors (all true) about Democrat John Edwards fathering a child with a campaign staffer. It's a double standard Republicans have learned to live with, but never was the media bias more shameless than in Campaign 2008—a political circus for the ages.

CHAPTER 3

O BAMA WAS A VERSATILE campaigner. He could play the arrogant professor or the preacher in a revival tent. He could play it hip, folksy, or too-cool-for-school. It's hard to decide which was most grating.

When it came time to play the race card, he played it folksy: "We know what kind of campaign they're gonna run. They're gonna try to make you afraid. They're gonna try to make you afraid of…*me*! [laughter] They're gonna say, you know what, he's, he's, he's, young…and inexperienced…and he's got a funny name. And did I mention…he's black?" [uproarious laughter].

It is curious that the man so widely billed as "postracial" would interject race directly into the campaign. The McCain team never once raised the issue of race; Obama did it all by his lonesome. In fact, McCain practically contorted himself into a pretzel to avoid any discussion of race.

In politics, as in society, the word *racism* is tossed around all too casually. Once a reputation has been tarnished by an allegation of racism, it's nearly impossible to remove the stain. Playing the race card was part of a premeditated strategy: Obama's handlers knew the remarks would generate sympathetic media coverage and put his opponent on the defensive. For the duration of the campaign, Obama effectively inoculated himself from attack. The maneuver worked brilliantly.

McCain was the perfect foil for his rival's race baiting. A klutzy campaigner under the best of circumstances, the Arizonan was visibly frustrated by the charismatic young senator. Obama's knack for adjusting his positions when it was politically convenient, and the media's refusal to call him on it, only complicated McCain's challenge. It brought to mind an old man chasing a fly around with a newspaper.

On one hand, McCain could go on the offensive against Obama, as he would have against any other inexperienced (and clearly unqualified) opponent. Alternatively, he could wage a muffled, dumbed-down campaign and hope for a lucky break.

The Republican opted for the latter approach. We're all living with the outcome.

Forget race; Obama's vulnerabilities could have never withstood scrutiny on a presidential level. That such devastating liabilities wouldn't be thoroughly investigated and exposed by the national media is unconscionable. As the campaign wound down, McCain treated his opponent with kid gloves, partly to avoid allegations of racism, and partly out of a sense of honor.

McCain is a product of an era in which honor meant something, but the veteran was dreaming if he believed the gesture would be reciprocated. Lurking just beneath the veneer of "hope and change" lay the Chicago political machine: corrupt, greedy, and ready to unleash its socialist nightmare upon the nation.

EARLY ON, OBAMA PLEDGED to tour the country with McCain in a series of town hall meetings. By the fall, the Democrat reneged on his commitment. If the Obama camp had its way, the candidate would be placed in as few unscripted venues as possible.

Obama's overreliance on scripted formats was evident during a forum hosted by Pastor Rick Warren at Saddleback Church, shortly before the parties' nominating conventions. One of the questions concerned abortion, a topic both candidates knew was coming.

"At what point does a baby get human rights, in your view?" asked Warren.

McCain: "At the moment of conception."

Obama: "Well, you know, I, uh, uh, think that, whether...you're looking at it from a theological perspective, or, uh, a scientific perspective, uh, answering that question with specificity, uh, uh, you know, is, is, uh, above my pay grade. But, but, but, but, but, but, let me, let me, let me just speak more generally about the issue of abortion, 'cause this is something I, obviously, the country wrestles with."

Obama's stammering, stuttering performance shocked anyone who hadn't seen the senator *sans* teleprompters. The comparisons with McCain's bold and confident responses to Warren's questions weren't lost on anyone. McCain's performance was so powerful, in fact, that Obama partisans accused the church of rigging the forum. It was a laughable charge, disproved since. The lesson from the debate, simply put, was that the Republicans had the more qualified candidate. Perhaps Obama, again unable to think and speak on his feet, wasn't quite the intellectual titan he'd been made out to be?

Privately, Democratic strategists panicked. The forum was limited to cable and evangelical Christian networks, but three more debates were scheduled closer to the election, each of which would draw millions more viewers than the Saddleback event. Obama's handlers scrambled to better prepare their man for the next round of debates, lest McCain make mincemeat out of him before a truly national audience. (Thus, ironically, Obama's disastrous performance at Saddleback was the wake-up call which may have saved his campaign.)

Speak forcefully, instructed his debate coaches. Act serious. Memorize your mini-speeches. No more "lawyerly, scholarly" (i.e., rambling, disorganized) responses. And scrap the cutesy one-liners ("above my pay grade") which impart an unpreparedness to be president.

Outside the debates, Obama's staff kept him in front of friendly crowds, taking only softball questions at carefully orchestrated events. At each appearance, campaign workers selected a diversity of audience members to sit behind the candidate (in one awkward moment, two Muslim women in headscarves were asked not to sit within camera range of Obama).

Like a Vegas magician, the campaign relied on stagecraft and imagery like never before—and oh, did it excel at it.

In an unprecedented display of chutzpah, Obama made the decision to deliver his acceptance speech in the open air at Invesco Field, home of the NFL's Denver Broncos. Even a spacious convention hall wasn't large enough to contain his supersized ego. The entire Democratic Convention was moved to the massive football stadium to accommodate more than eighty thousand party faithful.

The move was an enormous gamble. Despite millions of prayers and rain dances, the weather cooperated.

Obama's much-ballyhooed address was held on the final night of the convention, August 28. The media were rapturous. The extravaganza was intended to give the appearance of Obama as a Greek god descending from Olympus (you really can't make this stuff up). The stage was decked out like an ancient Greek temple, complete with pillars. All that was missing was the toga.

To those of us at home, the spectacle was more of a Greek tragedy. It brought to mind *hubris*, the Greek word meaning pride before a fall. At least the bloggers had fun with it. One wrote about the "Obamessiah" coming to "Obamapolis" to save mankind. Another deadpanned, "They must have thought a manger, sheep, and three wise men would have been too gaudy."

By contrast, McCain delivered his acceptance speech in front of stars and stripes.

As Obama spoke beside those phony Greek columns, I marveled at the cult of personality on display before the nation—no, the *world*. These folks must have been drinking some powerful Kool-Aid.

THE DAY AFTER THE MOUNT OLYMPUS stunt, it was McCain's turn to make history. The Grand Old Party nominee tapped Sarah Palin, the little-known governor of Alaska, as his running mate.

The selection was a jolt of rocket fuel for the colorless McCain campaign. Conservatives were instantly energized. The logjam was broken; money and volunteer resources now flowed freely to the Republican cause. Palin was just the second woman to be named to the national ticket of a major party, and the first-ever Republican woman. Considering Obama's dismissive treatment of Hillary Clinton during his primary, Republicans were hoping the selection would rally female voters around the McCain/Palin ticket.

Liberals were mortified by the surprise pick. This successful, articulate, attractive, conservative woman was the embodiment of everything so reviled by the far left. "*That woman*," as they took to deriding her, represented a very real threat to the Anointed One—and they knew it.

The Democrats' reaction was an amalgam of fear, shock, anger, and resentment. It was unbecoming to watch grown men, some with creditable careers in politics and journalism, throwing hissy fits on national television. The left and the media were determined to carry their man over the finish line. They'd invested far too much of their time, emotion, and prestige in Obama. He was the embodiment of "too big to fail."

They say adversity reveals character. In its no-holds-barred assault against Sarah Palin and her family, the American left revealed its lack thereof.

The first line of attack was that Palin was too inexperienced to be one heartbeat away from the presidency. Democrats, having nominated the least experienced major-party candidate in the last hundred years, were clearly grasping at straws. If Palin was unqualified for the Oval Office, what exactly was Obama?

For the record, let's compare the credentials of Sarah Palin, the number-two person on the Republican ticket, to those of Barack Obama, the top man on the Democratic side. We'll begin with Obama:

- Started out as an inner-city "community organizer."
- Obtained a law degree from Harvard. Served as president of the Harvard Law Review, a largely figurehead position; left a scant paper trail and was never published.
- Part-time lecturer at the University of Chicago, during which time he taught three courses per year.
- Junior partner at a law firm during the 1990s. Tried no cases.
- No private sector or executive experience.
- State senator, 1997-2004. No major accomplishments to speak of; frequently voted "present" in lieu of taking positions on controversial issues.
- United States Senator, 2004-2008. Spent his entire tenure running for president.

And now, Palin:

- Started out as a sports reporter, helped with her husband's commercial fishing business, and owned a snowmobile, watercraft, and ATV business. Has experience in the private sector.
- Two terms on the Wasilla City Council, 1992-1996.
- Two terms as mayor of Wasilla. Defeated the incumbent by campaigning against wasteful city spending. Cut property taxes by 75 percent.
- Elected president of the Alaska Conference of Mayors.
- Chairman of the Alaska Oil & Gas Conservation Commission.
- Elected governor of Alaska in 2006, defeating an incumbent Republican. Became its first female and youngest-ever governor. Has executive experience.
- Enjoyed the highest approval ratings of any governor in the country.

Advantage: Palin. Her experience trumps Obama's, and she's delivered more than just speeches.

CHAPTER 4

OBAMA SUPPORTERS COULD BE downright mean. Their offensive against Palin's teenage children revealed an incivility heretofore unseen in presidential politics. In years past, personal attacks against candidates' family members, and especially minor children, were verboten. During the 1990s, the Clintons asked that their daughter's privacy be respected, and to a person, the press and political opponents complied. The attacks on the Palin family were gutter politics at their worst.

This may explain why even twelve- and thirteen-year-old children became so openly hostile during the 2008 campaign. They were parroting the behavior and attitudes of their elders. Of all the presidential elections in my lifetime, I'd never witnessed such polarization, especially among my students. I was appalled by the taunting that took place the morning after the election. Several Obama backers reduced one young girl to tears for her support of the McCain/Palin campaign.

Reports of property damage against McCain backers were common. Vandals in Florida caused $4,500 worth of damage to a doctor's car which sported a "Nobama" sticker. This was hardly an isolated incident. I personally knew McCain supporters who forwent yard signs and bumper stickers out of fear of vandalism. In every election there are scattered reports of opponents' signs being stolen, but never before have so many criminal acts been committed in the "advocacy" of one candidate.

From any objective standpoint, it is difficult to explain the near-godlike status imparted to this ordinary politician. Several of my middle-school students sported Obama tee shirts, caps, and jewelry. One youngster even wore basketball shoes with Obama's name and face emblazoned on them. I finally had to inquire about his impassioned support for the Democratic nominee.

In a very neutral manner, I asked him, "What is it about Obama you like so much?"

He took a deep breath and thought for a minute. I wasn't trying to put him on the spot, but I figured he could surely come up with *something*. Finally, the young man shrugged. "I just think he'll be good for America," was his reply.

I let it go at that. I really couldn't blame him; even most adults would be unable to answer. After all, the media had soaked the nation with the pro-Obama message for two excruciating years. He plays basketball! He knows rap stars! He did a YouTube video! His wife goes sleeveless! They do fist bumps! There was no escaping it, and the young were especially susceptible to the hype.

One blogger wrote that she hadn't witnessed such a phenomenon since the Beatles descended upon America. Like the Beatles, Obama was a performer. Except the Beatles weren't running to be president of the United States.

An insightful colleague helped put the whole matter into perspective. Just months after the Kennedy assassination, the Beatles won the hearts of a grieving nation. The year 2008 was also a difficult period for the country: the economy was in free fall, people were losing their homes, and our military was engaged in two wars with uncertain outcomes. Americans were depressed, nervous, and angry.

My colleague summarized the Obama-mania this way: "The nation was yearning for a hero, so they made one up."

LISTENING TO AN OBAMA SPEECH is like swallowing a spoonful of sugar. It tastes good going down, but lacks any real nutritional value. That soaring rhetoric, brimming with platitudes but devoid of substance, was enough to win over impressionable voters like my young seatmate at the Las Vegas rally, and millions like her. One Republican strategist remarked, with grudging admiration: "He says nothing better than anybody."

Considering how much Obama loves to speak, it is odd that we learned so little about him during the course of the campaign. Obama was a media creation, yet he was, in many ways, a stealth candidate. That's the great paradox.

McCain's life was an open book; he's been a public figure dating back to Vietnam. Yet for all we knew about the Republican nominee, just as little was known about Obama. (We'll rectify that in the pages ahead.)

Has there ever been a candidate who remained such an enigma to the American people? The stakes couldn't have been higher, but come Election Day, voters were forced to render a verdict without all the facts. *Just trust us,* said the media. *Take our word for it.*

Questions about Obama's background were deemed a "distraction." Skeptics were mean-spirited and intolerant. Obama's leadership, we were told, would restore our society to greatness. His oratory could soothe our broken spirit. His election would atone for our sins. The

United States could take its place amongst the enlightened nations of the world once more.

Such was the media narrative.

"Change You Can Believe In" was Obama's well-worn campaign slogan. "Just Take Our Word For It" might have been more apropos.

There was at least one notable exception. In October, a reporter with WFTV, Orlando's ABC affiliate, asked Biden whether his running mate was a closet Marxist. Expecting another powder-puff interview, Biden stumbled through his response ("I don't know who's writing your questions," and "Are you joking?"). The reporter was pilloried afterward, and the station received this terse communication from the Obama campaign: "Further opportunities for your station to interview with this campaign are unlikely, at best for the duration of the remaining days until the election."

Give her credit: it's the job of the media to conduct hard-hitting interviews—and frankly, that very question was on the minds of millions of Americans. That a reporter dared to inquire about Obama's ideology actually became a news story itself.

Marxist or not, the president's ideology is a far cry from the moderate, reassuring tone he struck throughout the election. It wasn't until after the inauguration that the nation beheld the radical agenda of its new commander in chief. We've since learned that Obama believes in big government, class warfare, and economic redistribution—with his cronies doling out the goods.

Who was the most fiscally conservative president since World War II? That answer is easy: Ronald Reagan. But who comes in second? Strange as it sounds: Bill Clinton. Obviously, that wouldn't have been the case but for the Republicans winning control of Congress in 1994, and forcing Clinton's hand on budget cuts, welfare reform, and capital gains tax reductions. (George W. Bush, a social conservative and an all-around decent man, wasn't a deficit hawk by any means. That's a notable blemish on his otherwise creditable legacy.)

That portrait of the moderate, Clintonian Democrat was still on voters' minds by 2008. Obama's messages of fiscal responsibility and economic populism resonated with independents, Reagan Democrats, and other swing voters. And then came the bait and switch. The Obama campaign was the ultimate Trojan horse.

When all the ballots were counted, Barack Obama captured 52.9 percent of the popular vote. He proceeded to govern as though he'd won 100 percent.

SERVING AS PRESIDENT FEEDS Obama's prodigious appetite for adulation and glorification. Even two years into his presidency, he was still locked into campaign mode, the adoring crowds fueling his insatiable psyche. Whenever difficult work beckoned, off he journeyed, delivering his trademark stem-winders, drawing energy from the masses. This pathological need for affirmation would make for an interesting analysis.

Liberal commentator Bill Maher said of Obama, "You don't have to be on television every minute of every day. You're the president, not a rerun of *Law & Order*."

The man is ubiquitous; even his handlers have worried about the nation suffering Obama fatigue. One Sunday, the president appeared on a record five morning news programs, including ABC, CBS, NBC, CNN, and Univision, to talk about health care.

Notably absent from his itinerary that particular weekend was Fox News Sunday, in spite of the cable news giant's titanic ratings. Obama's vendetta against Fox News borders on the obsessive. While he has grown accustomed to kid-gloves treatment from most corners of the media, Fox has consistently asked the tough questions. (Its reporters were kicked off Obama's campaign jet as punishment.) This president needs to have his ego stroked, and when someone won't play along, it becomes personal.

Since his inaugural, Obama hasn't grown into the job; in many ways, his stature has diminished. While past presidents have endeavored to stay above the fray, Obama's willingness to get down in the muck with opponents and even media personalities is highly unstatesmanlike. This goes beyond mere pettiness; this is the kind of passive-aggressive behavior that lands wayward teens in counseling. It is possible that Obama's renowned arrogance actually masks a much deeper insecurity.

CHAPTER 5

Owing to his upbringing, Barack Obama doesn't view the United States as most of us do: as a liberator, a beacon of freedom, and the greatest force for good the world has ever known. He doesn't subscribe to Reagan's "shining city on the hill" analogy; too strong were his family and childhood influences.

The dominant figures during Obama's formative years were his Caucasian mother and grandparents. The stories of these and other important influences in Obama's youth are truly fascinating, but they garnered only superficial coverage in the run-up to the election. Their echoes can be heard in the walls of the White House today.

Obama's maternal grandfather, Stanley Dunham, lived through a tragedy no child should ever imagine: at age eight, he found the body of his mother, who'd taken her own life. Abandoned by their father, Stanley and his brother were sent off to live with their grandparents. Young Stanley developed a rebellious streak: he punched his principal and was kicked out of school. He found a future as a furniture salesman, and it was said that he could "charm the legs off a couch" (the apple must not fall far from the tree). Dunham enlisted in the U.S. Army during World War II.

Obama's grandmother, Madelyn Lee Payne Dunham, had a more conventional upbringing. Against the wishes of her parents, she married Stanley shortly before the war. In later years, Madelyn worked her way up to become one of the first female vice presidents at the Bank of Hawaii. Her advancement was hard-fought, and Obama has frequently cited her struggles as an example of sex discrimination. However, it is more likely (and rather ironic) that she was the victim of reverse discrimination: a generation ago in Hawaii, it was extremely difficult for whites to move up the corporate ladder.

Stanley Dunham desperately wanted a son, but the couple's only child turned out to be a daughter. Ever the rebel, Stanley gave her a boy's name anyway; he actually named his daughter after himself. Young Stanley was taunted about her name throughout her childhood. By the time she went to college, she simply went by her middle name, Ann.

It was during her adolescence on Mercer Island, near Seattle, Washington, that her worldview began to take shape. In the late 1950s, a conservative era in American history, Ann developed a rebellious streak of her own, one that would exceed even that of her father. She attended Mercer Island High School, whose staff included several openly Marxist teachers. The chairman of the Mercer Island school board testified before Congress that he was a member of the Communist Party.

A teenage Ann Dunham came under the influence of two radical teachers who urged students to challenge societal norms and question authority. She was required to read *The Communist Manifesto* and other pro-Marxist literature. So steeped was the school in the Marxist philosophy that the hallway between the two classrooms was dubbed "anarchy alley."

The teachers encouraged students to question the existence of God and the traditional family. It was then that Ann declared herself an atheist. Classmates described her as a "fellow traveler" and "the original feminist."

The Dunhams moved to Hawaii in 1960, but Mercer Island High School never left Ann. She took the unusual step of enrolling, at the height of the Cold War, in a Russian-language class at the University of Hawaii. It was there that she met her husband-to-be, Barack Hussein Obama, a Muslim socialist from Kenya. Barely out of high school, Ann was captivated by this older, worldly man.

She was just eighteen years old and three months pregnant when she eloped to Maui with Barack. Her mother opposed the union, but this was Ann, challenging authority. She was reportedly unaware that her new husband was still married to his Kenyan wife.

EVERYONE HAS HEARD THE STORY of Obama's growing up in Hawaii, born on August 4, 1961 to a Muslim man from Kenya and a mother with (to put it delicately) an erratic streak.

The president has called his mother the dominant figure in his formative years. "The values she taught me continue to be my touchstone when it comes to how I go about the world of politics," he has said. The radical influences of her high school years were surely passed on from mother to son.

Barack Sr. deserted the family shortly thereafter. He returned to Kenya and later died, an alcoholic. Ann remarried a student from Indonesia, Lolo Soetoro, another Muslim. The family then relocated to Indonesia, where young Barack would spend his elementary school years. He'd welcome a half-sister, Maya, in 1970.

When he was ten, Barack was sent back to Hawaii to live with his grandparents for reasons that aren't entirely clear. His mother would live a somewhat nomadic existence, ducking in and out of his life over the next several years. Suffice it to say, stability was not a hallmark of Obama's childhood.

Little else is known about Obama's grandparents, Stanley and Madelyn Dunham. In Seattle, they belonged to a Unitarian church which came to be known as "The Little Red Church on the Hill" for its communist influences. In Hawaii, Stanley befriended one Franklin Marshall Davis, identified as "Frank" in Obama's memoirs, and encouraged him to mentor Barack.

Davis was an open communist who preached that American capitalism is responsible for imperialism, class struggles, and an exploitation of workers. Years earlier, his activities caught the attention of the FBI and anticommunist congressional committees. One of the few African-American men living in Hawaii in the 1970s, "Frank" became something of a father figure to the teenage Obama. The details of their relationship are murky, but it is believed that Davis, a onetime community organizer himself, introduced the young man to his future vocation.

The closest thing to a conservative influence in Obama's early years was his Caucasian grandmother. Once more, we have little to go by— Obama's autobiographies contain little accurate source material—but it's likely that she was the only person in his childhood who ever said no to him. That's a word rarely heard by Obama, even as an adult, and may go a long way toward explaining his sense of entitlement.

Whether Obama harbored resentments toward his grandmother will never be known, but the question surfaced during the Democratic primaries. In his heralded speech on race at the height of the Jeremiah Wright controversy, Obama's depiction of Madelyn Dunham raised eyebrows: "I can no more disown him [Rev. Wright] than I can my white grandmother, a woman who helped raise me, a woman who sacrificed again and again for me, a woman who loves me as much as she loves anything in this world—but a woman who once confessed her fear of black men who passed by her on the street, and who on more than one occasion has uttered racial or ethnic stereotypes that made me cringe."

Obama expounded tersely on his remarks by referring to his grandmother as a "typical white person." The comment barely stirred a breeze. Had any other candidate—certainly a Republican—spoken of a "typical black person," he or she would have been lambasted for it, and rightly so. His or her political career would have been over.

The deeper meaning of Obama's remarks is best left to speculation. What is apparent is that his relationship with his grandmother was complex. When his campaign was in peril, he invoked her name, and it was not in the most charitable light.

Madelyn Dunham, who unwittingly became a part of the narrative, wouldn't live to see her grandson ascend to the presidency. She passed away the day before the election.

LIKE MANY TEENAGERS GROWING UP in the 1970s, Obama experimented with alcohol, marijuana, and cocaine, the use of which he has described as his greatest moral failure. He admitted to confusion over his racial identity during high school and took to calling himself "Barry."

Considering the circumstances of his upbringing, Obama deserves credit for providing an intact family for his daughters. Many adults from similar backgrounds might have taken a self-destructive turn. If he's been a positive role model for young men from broken homes or disadvantaged backgrounds, we can only tip our hats.

Obama's devotion to his family is most likely the result of his grandparents' influence. His ideology, on the other hand, was almost certainly inherited from his mother.

Ann Dunham's story ended sadly. At age fifty, after finally earning her Ph.D., she attended Barack and Michelle's wedding. Two years later, the first signs of ovarian cancer appeared. A globetrotter to the end, she was misdiagnosed by an Indonesian doctor, who believed she was suffering from indigestion. By the time her condition was properly diagnosed, it was too late.

Stanley Ann Dunham Soetoro passed away in 1995, well before her son's rise to prominence. Through him, her worldview lives on.

CHAPTER 6

O BAMA WAS INDEED HIS mother's son. His early adulthood was spent wandering, drifting, and generally leading a vagabond existence. He made several stops academically and professionally, searching for his place in the world, but rarely leaving fingerprints along the way. For such an international megastar, his paper trail is strikingly thin.

After high school, Obama left the relative security of Hawaii for the mainland. Like most college students, he had no particular plan for his life at this point. Like many of his peers, he fell under the influence of campus radicals and Marxist professors.

His first stop was Occidental College in Los Angeles, "Oxy," as it's known. After two years he embarked upon another major life change, abruptly moving across the country to attend Columbia University in New York. We don't know why he chose to leave Occidental; in fact, we know next to nothing about this period in Obama's life.

In his first book, *Dreams from My Father,* Obama touched on his years at Oxy, providing an intriguing but all-too-brief glimpse into his background:

"To avoid being mistaken for a sellout, I chose my friends carefully. The more politically active black students. The foreign students. The Chicanos. The Marxist professors and structural feminists and punk-rock performance poets."

His memoirs reveal little else about his college days. Like detectives, we're forced to piece together the few clues we have available. Even then, the picture is hazy.

We do know that as an undergraduate, Obama traveled to Pakistan for three weeks with a college friend whose family was from Karachi, that nation's largest city. Pakistan was an unusual destination for Americans; for most twenty-year-olds of modest means, it would have been the adventure of a lifetime. Curiously, his two autobiographies make no mention of the trip, and he's rarely spoken of it since.

For many of us, college was the most memorable experience of our lives, yet the Obama narrative all but erases those years out of existence. How did his friends, professors, and coursework shape his outlook on life? What was his class rank? How did the trip to Pakistan contribute to his worldview? How did he pay for his education? Did he benefit from affirmative action at any time?

Why has he chosen not to discuss this period in his life? These are all reasonable questions.

Obama has also been unwilling to release any of his university records. For better or worse, presidential contenders are held to intense public and private scrutiny; they are exposed, in the words of Lincoln, "warts and all." Most have voluntarily disclosed their university transcripts. Other times, the media have trolled for records of a candidate's academic performance.

When Bush described himself as a C student, his detractors laughed. Even Bush poked fun at himself ("To the C students, I say, 'You too can be president of the United States!' "). Then it was revealed that Al Gore's grades were about the same, and John Kerry's even worse.

For candidates in recent times, full disclosure has become something of a rite of passage—except in the case of Obama. He has refused to unseal his records at Occidental, Columbia, or Harvard Law School. Should anyone care?

In this instance, we have a right to know. For possibly the first time in history, we were told to look past a candidate's lack of experience; we were to focus instead on his biography and personality. But a very large part of that biography remains shrouded in mystery.

"It's his right to keep his records sealed," argue Obama partisans. From a strictly legal standpoint, they are correct. The problem is that we have so little else to go by. His insistence on secrecy begs the obvious question: why?

To add to the mystery, Obama kept a very low profile at Columbia.

Fox News contacted four hundred students who attended Columbia University at the same time as Obama, but none could remember meeting him. Obama's photograph isn't in the school's yearbook, and he refuses to talk (or write) about his undergraduate days. The school's valedictorian, Wayne Allyn Root, who also graduated in 1983, said, "I never met him in my life and don't know anyone who ever did."

THE YEAR 1985 FOUND Barack Obama living in New York City, working a series of mundane jobs and figuring out what to do with his life. He'd graduated from Columbia a couple years earlier, but with a degree in political science, his career options were limited. Frank Davis had been a community organizer in Chicago years before. Perhaps the thought of following in his mentor's footsteps intrigued Obama?

The graduate answered a want ad placed by the Developing Communities Project (DCP), which needed to fill a community organizing position in Chicago. Obama interviewed for the position, wowed them with his personality, and the job was his. Relocation was old hat to the much-traveled twenty-four-year-old, who had now claimed residence in the nation's three largest cities.

The pay was meager, but Obama's motives transcended financial considerations. Having been steeped in leftist traditions since child-hood, he saw community organizing as a means of helping the under-privileged—or, as Davis likely characterized them, those exploited and left behind by our greedy capitalist system.

Halfway around the world, Ann Dunham had to be smiling.

But Obama also nursed his own career ambitions. Organizing the inner city would gain him street cred with local politicians, establish his liberal bona fides, and build a base for a future political campaign. To the young aspirant, the job was a win-win situation.

The DCP assigned Obama to organize predominantly black, inner-city neighborhoods on Chicago's South Side. It was here that he became engrossed in the teachings of the late Saul Alinsky. The two never met (Alinsky died in 1972) but the community organizing pioneer would have a more profound effect on Obama than any single person in his life, save for his family.

The DCP adhered to Alinsky's model of community organizing, which was laid out in his signature publication, *Rules for Radicals*. Alinsky was widely recognized as an organizational genius, and *Rules for Radicals* has been described as the blueprint for a bloodless socialist revolution. Obama studied it, and oh, did he learn it well.

Published the year before Alinsky's death, *Rules for Radicals* is the sacred writ of community organizing. The author makes no bones about his mission. His book opens with a clear admonition: "What follows is for those who want to change the world from what it is to what they believe it should be. *The Prince* was written by Machiavelli for the

Haves on how to hold power. *Rules for Radicals* is written for the Have-Nots on how to take it away."

Per Alinsky's model, "community organizing" is code for community agitating. He urges organizers to "rub raw the sores of discontent" and to convince their communities that government, corporations, and the wealthy are responsible for their suffering. Once the people have been sufficiently agitated, organizers train the community to bond together and flex its political muscle.

Alinsky's rules call on community organizers to "pick the target, freeze it, personalize it, and polarize it." He designates buzzwords and phrases to be used, including "common welfare" and "pursuit of happiness." Make a minority look like the majority. Get in peoples' faces. Like Machiavelli's prince, Alinsky makes clear that the end justifies the means. To win debates, demonize your opponent; when presented with facts, respond with ambiguities; when talking to groups, speak in platitudes. Most importantly, leave everyone believing you're on his or her side.

For anyone paying attention to Campaign 2008, that playbook ought to sound eerily familiar.

Alinsky himself was a confirmed atheist, but he viewed inner-city churches as the ideal infrastructure for his brand of community organizing. At this point in his life, Obama was, religiously, an agnostic; this proved troublesome when working side-by-side with pastors and church members. To maximize his effectiveness as an organizer, Obama realized he would have to join a church.

He didn't fool around. He headed straight for the largest, most influential church on Chicago's South Side, Trinity United Church of Christ. There, he'd meet his spiritual adviser, the infamous Jeremiah Wright.

Obama soaked up Alinsky's teachings like a sponge, calling them "the best education I ever had." He showed a natural gift for the craft of the preacher. Obama could be probing, and then charismatic; he could foment anger, and then offer hope. Twenty years later, those abilities vaulted him into the Oval Office.

Ultimately, the South Side remained much as it was before Obama swooped in: poor, crime-ridden, and bereft of jobs or industry. Welfare dependency, fatherless children, and drug addiction are just as rampant there today as then. Children remain trapped in a monolithic public school system that offers little in the way of opportunity. Obama may have succeeded in delivering a few more votes for the Chicago Democratic machine, but his communities were hardly transformed.

After four years as a community organizer, making barely minimum wage, the ambitious young man was ready to take his talents to a larger stage. In 1988, it was on to Harvard Law School and the next chapter in his life.

Obama managed to rack up seventeen parking tickets during law school. He paid exactly two of them. The remaining fifteen were unpaid until he launched his presidential bid nearly two decades later.

OBAMA WAS NAMED PRESIDENT of the Harvard Law Review, an achievement the media went to great lengths to trumpet. In truth, it was more of a figurehead position. After law school, he briefly returned to community activism. In 1992, Obama directed Project Vote, an ACORN (Association of Community Organizations for Reform Now) partner which registered 150,000 African-Americans across Illinois to vote.

By the mid-1990s, he was slogging away as a junior partner at a Chicago law firm. The Harvard graduate found himself researching the law and writing memos, but despite the oratorical brilliance he'd demonstrate in later years, the firm didn't assign him to try any cases.

During this period, he was a part-time instructor at the University of Chicago, teaching three courses in constitutional law per year. According to the school, Obama's title was "senior lecturer"; he was not a "professor of law," as is often reported. He spent a total of twelve years at the university, but never published any academic writings.

The gigs were mundane and unfulfilling. Obama hungered for something more. Recently married, his political resumé was beginning to take shape. Through an odd twist of fate, he'd make his first foray into the decidedly more glamorous world of politics.

Obama won his first campaign in 1996. He ran unopposed, but that had nothing to do with charm and charisma. He won his race the Chicago way: by having his opponents kicked off the ballot.

CHAPTER 7

ALICE PALMER REPRESENTED THE South Side in the Illinois Senate from 1991 to early 1997. Her politics might be alien to most of us, but she fit right in with the Chicago machine.

Palmer previously served as an executive board member for the U.S. Peace Council, which had been identified by the FBI as a communist front group. She traveled to Moscow to attend the Twenty-seventh Congress of the Communist Party of the Soviet Union in 1986. Following the trip, Palmer wrote an article for the Communist Party USA's newspaper in which she extolled the virtues of the Soviet system— shortly before the fall of the Soviet Union.

In 1995, Congressman Mel Reynolds was forced to resign from the U.S. House of Representatives following a sex scandal involving an underage campaign worker (there's never a dull moment in Chicago politics). Palmer decided to run for Reynolds's vacant seat in a special election to be held that November.

Fully anticipating victory, she designated the thirty-four-year-old Obama, who'd made a name for himself in local circles after his ambitious Project Vote effort, as her successor in the state senate. Palmer went so far as to introduce the up-and-comer to her circle of liberal backers and party elders. Among them were former Weather Underground terrorists Bill Ayers and Bernardine Dohrn. The event, which marked the formal kickoff of Barack Obama's political career, was actually held at the Ayerses' home.

One wonders why the communist-sympathizing Palmer would promote Obama as her successor. Did he beguile her with his charm? Or did she see shades of herself in her young apprentice?

In any event, Palmer overestimated her own political fortunes as well as Obama's loyalties. Palmer was trounced by Jesse Jackson Jr. in the special election to succeed Reynolds. Meanwhile, Obama was lustily campaigning for her seat.

Obama went so far as to seek (and receive) the endorsement of the Chicago New Party. The New Party was a political coalition formed in 1992 with the intention of "fusing" members from sundry leftist organizations: ACORN, the Democratic Socialists of America, the Communist Party USA, and the like.

Still smarting from the special election defeat, Palmer made a late decision to seek re-election to her old senate seat. She announced her intentions shortly before the filing deadline, and her campaign scrambled to gather the necessary signatures to qualify her for the primary ballot. But qualify she did, and Democratic leaders asked Obama to bow out in deference to the incumbent.

But Obama refused; he'd learned a thing or two about hardball politics from his community organizing days. He knew he couldn't defeat Palmer in a head-to-head matchup, so he arranged to have her thrown off the ballot.

How does one go about having an opponent disqualified? Obama set out to challenge the signatures on Palmer's nominating petition. His supporters went through the signatures, one by one, moving to strike hundreds of names. By the time they were through, Palmer was left about two hundred signatures short of qualifying for the ballot. (There were two lesser-known candidates who qualified for the primary; Obama's team had them knocked off as well.)

Many of the names were invalidated due to technicalities. For instance, if the person collecting the signatures had not been registered specifically to perform the task, any signatures he or she collected could be stricken. Likewise, if a name was printed—not in cursive—that signature was tossed out.

Thus, the primary was down to Barack Obama versus…nobody. Since the Republican Party is a nonentity on the South Side, winning the Democratic primary was tantamount to victory. Asked if he had done voters a disservice by eliminating the competition, Obama's response was rich: "I think they ended up with a very good state senator."

Neither Mel Reynolds nor Alice Palmer will be missed, but they each altered the course of history. Without their scandal and ineptitude, respectively, the nation might never have heard of Barack Obama.

To its credit, CNN ran a fairly hard-hitting piece on the Obama-Palmer imbroglio. Otherwise, the story was ignored throughout the presidential campaign. Obama was the new Sir Galahad, and the media weren't about to sully that image.

WHAT ABOUT BILL AYERS, the former domestic terrorist in whose home Obama launched his first political campaign?

Ayers co-founded the Weather Underground (or Weathermen) in 1969. A young Obama supporter wouldn't have heard of the Weather Underground; he'd probably assume it was a hip rock band that performs at global-warming rallies. In reality, the organization has a radical, violent history. As self-described communist revolutionaries, the members embraced violence as a means of protest against the Vietnam War and on behalf of other militant causes. The Weather Underground was responsible for a series of bombings throughout the 1970s, including the Pentagon, the U.S. Capitol, and New York City police headquarters.

Ayers and Dohrn made the FBI's most-wanted list and were eventually caught. Unfortunately, the government's case against them was based on illegal wiretaps, so the charges were dismissed. Ayers did no jail time, while Dohrn served just seven months. The two were later married. Unrepentant to the end, Ayers famously declared, "I wish I had done more." He was pictured on the cover of *Chicago Magazine* standing on a crumpled American flag beneath the title, "No Repentance." That the man walks free is a miscarriage of justice.

Fast-forward to today, and Ayers boasts a cushy teaching position at the University of Illinois at Chicago, holding the titles "distinguished professor of education" and "senior university scholar." He also became a key player in the cesspool of Chicago politics, which is where the Obama relationship was born.

The Ayers connection came up all too briefly during the presidential race when Hillary Clinton's team raised the issue. Obama dismissed Ayers as just "a guy who lives in my neighborhood." Chief strategist David Axelrod, a veteran of Chicago politics himself, went several steps further, acknowledging that Obama and Ayers "have a very friendly relationship." Which is the truth?

The media never aggressively pursued the answer; the years-long association between the two was ignored, mischaracterized, or excused outright. Obama partisans rallied to his defense, though they couldn't have known the details of the relationship themselves. Some even mocked the controversy: Obama, a terrorist? He was just a child when Ayers was planting his bombs!

They miss the point. No one accused Obama of *being* a terrorist; he chose to *associate* with onetime terrorists. Obama's relationship with Ayers helped him climb the ladder in the world of Chicago politics. It started with his first campaign in 1996 and continued from that time.

Obama wrote a blurb in the *Chicago Tribune* in 1997 in praise of a book written by Ayers. The men served together on two boards, the Chicago Annenberg Challenge and the Woods Fund, kicking off an eight-year working relationship. Obama was savvy; he knew the friendship/association afforded him access to Ayers's sphere of influence within Democratic circles. The ambitious politico was getting his ticket punched.

His relationship with Ayers was relevant because it contradicted the postpartisan, nonideological image that was such a part of Obama's appeal. In fact, the associations with Ayers, Dohrn, and others would have disqualified Obama from obtaining a security clearance. He couldn't have gotten a job at the FBI.

(Imagine if a Republican had maintained a decade-long association with an unrepentant abortion clinic bomber. He would have lasted about two seconds as a viable presidential candidate.)

Was Obama a terrorist? Of course not. The question is unserious.

Did he approve of Ayers's criminal history? Absolutely not, and no one has suggested otherwise.

Do the men share common ideological ground? That's safe to say.

Did Obama develop a friendly relationship with Ayers in order to further his own political career? You bet he did.

Sarah Palin was criticized in the press for suggesting that Obama was "palling around with terrorists," but she was 100 percent right.

THE ANNENBERG FOUNDATION WAS established by the late billionaire Walter Annenberg with the intention of reforming public education throughout the country. In 1995, Ayers co-wrote a $49.2 million grant proposal to the foundation on behalf of Chicago public schools; he later stated that his objective was "radical" reform of the city's educational system. The grant was approved and, amid much fanfare, the Chicago Annenberg Challenge (CAC) was born. Ayers installed Obama as the first chairman of the board, and over the next six years they partnered to advance the CAC's far-left agenda. Curiously, Obama's autobiographies omit any reference to his leadership of the CAC.

Obama and Ayers also served together on the Woods Fund, which makes grants "for less advantaged people and communities," to quote its charter. The Woods Fund steered tens of millions of dollars to community organizing projects, including Obama's former employer, the DCP.

Two of these grants, totaling $75,000, were made to the Arab American Action Network, a controversial community-organizing group founded by Professor Rashid Khalidi. Another questionable Obama associate, Khalidi could charitably be described as a terror apologist. He was a spokesman for Yassir Arafat in the 1970s, has expressed support for Palestinian violence, and called Israel a destructive, racist state. Khalidi was well known in Chicago's Arab-American community. Obama, ever the politician, saw him as a friend and ally.

Khalidi held a fundraiser for Obama in 2000, the two taught at the University of Chicago at the same time, and Obama attended a farewell dinner for Khalidi in 2003. At that dinner—Khalidi was leaving to head the Middle East Studies Department at Columbia University—Obama spoke warmly about his friendship with the Khalidis. Other keynoters included Ayers himself and a host of rabidly anti-Israel, anti-American speakers.

The Obama-friendly *Los Angeles Times* obtained a videotape of the event but has refused to release it publicly. Is this another case of the media covering for their man? As a presidential candidate, Obama postured himself as a supporter of Israel. Could the contents of the tape have proved embarrassing?

We may never know all the details of the relationship between Rashid Khalidi and Barack Obama. Both men have refused to discuss it, and Khalidi stayed out of sight throughout the campaign, at one point hiding his face and scampering away from Fox News cameras. We do know that the two shared a friendship and, to some degree, an ideological affinity. It was another troubling Obama association that the media has decided is off-limits to discussion.

OBAMA'S RELATIONSHIP WITH ACORN dates back to his community agitating days. Through the Woods Fund, Obama provided generously for his comrades at the now-defunct organization, doling out millions in various grants. He has lectured at ACORN seminars and sued the state of Illinois on its behalf.

According to its mission statement, ACORN lobbied on a range of issues affecting working-class, minority, and low-income individuals. Unofficially, it was a left-wing, antibusiness protest group dedicated to political activism and wealth redistribution. Manhattan Institute scholar Sol Stern wrote that ACORN promoted "a 1960s-bred agenda of anticapitalism, central planning, victimology, and government handouts to the poor." The erstwhile organization received about 40 percent of its funding from the taxpayers.

ACORN demanded that lenders underwrite mortgages to unqualified home buyers in heavily minority neighborhoods, and then railed against those same banks when they were forced to foreclose. Its political activism was a principal contributor (along with the false inflation of home values) to the bursting of the real estate bubble and the subsequent economic fallout.

ACORN formally endorsed Obama, its once and future benefactor, for president in 2008. In turn, Obama hired a subsidiary of the organization to conduct his get-out-the-vote efforts. (This was not disclosed to the Federal Election Commission in a timely manner, as required by law. The Obama campaign called it a "clerical error." More likely, it was an attempt to hide the campaign's involvement with the controversial outfit until after the election.)

In their zeal to deliver votes for Obama, several ACORN chapters ran afoul of state and federal laws. The tax-exempt entity was under investigation in at least fifteen states for voter registration fraud. In 2008 alone, an estimated one-third of ACORN's voter registration cards turned out to be fake. ACORN workers registered one man seventy times and even registered a cat, along with scores of dead people. We may never know how many phantom votes were ultimately cast for Obama.

In Stamford, Connecticut, voter registrars rejected so many ACORN registration cards that their office incurred $20,000 in cost overruns. The FBI opened a criminal investigation into the matter, but the Obama Justice Department shut it down in March 2009.

The organization had its share of other legal troubles. In San Diego, an ACORN employee advised an undercover reporter on smuggling underage prostitutes across the border. Its Maryland chapter provided tax advice to journalists who were posing as a prostitute and a pimp. Amid scandal and mismanagement, ACORN was forced to formally disband in 2010. But don't count them out: look for its affiliates to re-emerge under new names and continue feasting at the public trough.

CHAPTER 8

AFTER LITERALLY ELIMINATING THE competition, Obama was elected to the Illinois Senate in 1996. He was re-elected in 1998 and 2002. Each time, he was unopposed in the primary and then faced token opposition in the general election. During his nearly eight years in Springfield, Obama compiled a consistently liberal voting record—few surprises there. What is intriguing about his tenure as a state lawmaker, however, was his habit of voting "present" on controversial measures.

Legislators may vote "yea" or "nay," but unbeknownst to most of their constituents, a third option is available in Illinois: a "present" vote. This affords a fallback for senators fearful of taking a stand on a divisive issue. In all, Obama voted "present" an incredible total of 129 times.

He cast a "present" vote on a bill to prosecute fifteen-year-olds as adults when they fire a gun on school grounds; only one senator voted against it. He voted "present" on a partial-birth abortion ban, and on a bill which protected the privacy of sex-abuse victims by having their trial records sealed (the latter passed the Senate unanimously). On legislation requiring strip clubs to be at least a thousand feet away from schools, daycare centers, and churches, Obama voted—drum roll please—"present."

The votes remain a mystery. It's difficult to see the upside, even to a nuanced politician like Obama, of equivocating on so many no-brainers. So much for courage and leadership. Obama's penchant for voting "present" was especially notable on the issue of abortion. He voted "present" on parental-consent legislation and then on a series of bills from 2001 to 2003 which came to be known as "Born Alive."

This requires some explanation.

In 1999, a Chicago-area nurse discovered that babies who survived induced-labor abortions at her hospital were being left to die in a soiled utility room. The babies, born alive and viable outside the womb, were kept out of view of patients and staff. The nurse, Jill Stanek, held one such baby for about forty-five minutes until his breathing ceased.

When the hospital refused to discontinue the practice, Stanek went public. The story made national news. In 2001, legislation was intro-duced in Illinois to require that hospital personnel make every effort to save the lives of babies who survive botched abortions.

The Born Alive legislation was assigned to the Senate Judiciary Committee, of which Obama was a minority member. He voted "nay" in committee, and then cast a "present" vote when the bill came before the full Senate. The legislation passed the Senate, but the session ended before the House of Representatives could follow suit.

When the bill was reintroduced in 2002, Obama voted "nay" both in committee and on the Senate floor. He was, in fact, the only senator to speak against passage of the legislation.

By 2003, Democrats had won control of the Illinois Senate, and this time, Born Alive was sent to the Health & Human Services Com-mittee—a notoriously liberal stronghold—chaired by Obama. He voted "nay" once again, and the bill died in his committee.

Apparently, back then the abortion issue wasn't above his pay grade.

Before you get too depressed, this story has a happy ending. In 2002, President Bush signed a virtually identical measure into law at the federal level. The "Born-Alive Infants Protection Act" ensures federal protection to any infant who survives a botched abortion procedure. The law passed the U.S. Senate by a vote of 98-0. Even liberals like Ted Kennedy, Hillary Clinton, and John Kerry voted in favor of the measure. That put Mr. Obama, then just a middling state legislator, to the left even of his own party on the fundamental issue of innocent human life.

OBAMA WOULDN'T TOIL IN anonymity for long. Casting tough votes may have intimidated him, but he wasn't bashful about ascending the political ladder. Bored with life in Springfield, Obama sought to move up the ranks, and fast.

From the moment he arrived at the state capital, Obama ingratiated himself with the body's power brokers, currying favors, toeing the party line, and generally paying his dues. He gained the attention of Emil Jones Jr., the Senate Democratic leader, who regarded Obama as a political star on the rise. Jones took the youngster under his wing and handed him relatively mundane legislation to shepherd through the body: increasing child care subsidies for low-income families, requiring notice to employees before plant closings, banning racial profiling by law enforcement, and so forth.

Obama's signature achievement was passage of campaign finance reform legislation, which banned lawmakers from using campaign funds for personal use and barred lobbyists from giving gifts to public officials. As he was fronting the measure for the powerful Jones, its passage was a foregone conclusion. Still, Obama frequently cited the law as evidence of his effectiveness as a legislator.

After just three years in the state senate, his ego was flourishing. When Obama looked in the mirror, he saw a United States congressman. His reflection wasn't so kind.

Obama declared his candidacy against U.S. Representative Bobby Rush in the Democratic primary to be held in March 2000. Toppling a sitting congressman is always a long shot, particularly in a primary, but the incumbent looked vulnerable. Rush had challenged Chicago Mayor Richard M. Daley in the mayoral election the previous year, and the results weren't pretty: Daley won 72 percent citywide and nearly carried the black vote. Obama smelled blood in the water.

It was a colossal miscalculation. Rush, a Baptist minister and veteran of the civil rights movement, crushed the young upstart by a better than two-to-one margin. Icarus had flown too close to the sun.

The incumbent had this to say about his challenger: "Barack Obama went to Harvard and became an educated fool."

The year 2000 was not kind to Obama. Fresh (so to speak) from his defeat, he flew to Los Angeles and applied for a floor pass to the Democratic National Convention. The application was denied.

OBAMA WAS USED TO getting his way, and the loss to Rush was a rare setback. All Obama would say afterward was, "He spanked me." He wouldn't be out for long, however.

In 2004, Peter Fitzgerald, a rather ordinary, one-term U.S. senator, announced that he wouldn't seek re-election for another term. That decision set off a mad scramble for the seat, and a sequence of events which were bizarre even by Illinois standards.

With Bush cruising at the top of the ticket, 2004 was expected to be a banner election year for Republicans. The party had its ideal senate candidate in Jack Ryan, a self-made millionaire who taught at an inner-city school. The ex-husband of actress Jeri Ryan, the Republican nominee was set to square off against the relatively unknown Democratic contender…Barack Obama!

Bet you didn't see that one coming.

From 1996 to 2004, Obama ran five different campaigns, one in each even-numbered year. Say what you will about the man, he loves politicking.

Obama outpaced six nondescript opponents to win the Democratic primary for the open seat. Endorsements from the state's three most powerful unions—the American Federation of State, County and Municipal Employees (AFSCME), the Service Employees International Union (SEIU), and the American Federation of Teachers (AFT)—effectively put him over the top. The endorsements marked the beginning of a hardy alliance between Obama and organized labor which continues to this day.

Ryan would be a formidable opponent in the general election. Now running statewide, had Obama once again bitten off more than he could chew? Possibly. Except that what happened to the Ryan campaign next is the stuff of soap operas.

Jack and Jeri Ryan had divorced five years earlier, and the *Chicago Tribune,* suspecting something juicy, sued to have their divorce records unsealed. The Ryans, who had a young son, agreed to release everything but the custody records. A judge ordered them released anyway. Sure enough, the records included Jeri's detailed allegations that her husband had taken her to sex clubs.

Game over.

Candidate Obama claimed that any "dirt" in the custody records should remain sealed—even as his supporters were clamoring for them to be released. With the Ryan campaign now history, the race was another cakewalk for Obama, who cemented his reputation as the luckiest politician in the cosmos. It was the second time a sex scandal helped pave the way for an Obama victory.

The Illinois GOP hastily installed conservative activist Alan Keyes as its nominee, but by then Obama's ticket to Washington was all but punched.

But wait! The twists kept coming.

IT WAS SENATOR JOHN KERRY of Massachusetts who unwittingly transformed Obama into an international celebrity.

Kerry, in the midst of an uphill battle against Bush, was failing miserably in his efforts to connect with the voters. The Democratic convention had all the makings of a snooze fest, so Kerry's team scrambled to find a keynote speaker who could breathe some life into the proceedings.

Obama, on the verge of becoming the only African-American in the U.S. Senate, found his way onto the short list. He wanted this badly: his aides lobbied Kerry's staff and even submitted an audition tape. Their persistence paid off. With polls showing the Democrats attracting less support from minority voters than in previous election cycles, Kerry selected Obama over the runner-up, Michigan Governor Jennifer Granholm. Obama was obviously an outside-the-box pick. In many ways, he was the anti-Kerry: young, hip, and energetic.

How's that for being in the right place at the right time?

Kerry was, at best, a lackluster candidate. Nature abhors a vacuum, so the convention buzz turned to the youthful keynoter with the unusual name. The day before his speech, crowds began following Obama around Boston. *This is rock-star treatment*, quipped one of his friends.

Obama, never at a loss for self-regard, rejoined: "Yeah, if you think it's bad today, wait until tomorrow...My speech is pretty good...I'm LeBron, baby. I can play on this level. I got some game!"

Give Obama credit: he's a gifted writer. On July 27, 2004, the heretofore unknown Chicagoan wowed his audience with a keynote address that stole the convention. The media could barely contain their euphoria.

Said Chris Matthews, prophetically: "That is an amazing moment in history right there...I have seen the first black president there."

"A phenom," declared the *Chicago Tribune*.

"After the speech last night...even if he had an opponent, he might get 100 percent of the vote," gushed Illinois Governor Rod Blagojevich.

Former Carter speechwriter Hendrick Hertzberg evidenced the media's almost childlike giddiness: "If he wrote that speech, then he should be president, because it's such a great speech."

For my part, I remember watching one network's fawning coverage of Obama's address (it may have been CNN) and thinking to myself, *"The media are going to make him president someday."*

I hate being right.

Obama showcased a swagger not seen since the appearance of the last Democratic president, Bill Clinton; in fact, it was widely agreed that he'd eclipsed his predecessor. He was the hottest thing since sunburn.

"There's not a liberal America and a conservative America, there's the United States of America. There's not a black America, and white America, and Latino America, and Asian America, there's the United States of America," was the catchphrase of the speech. The soothing platitudes belied the ideological dogmatism and partisanship which would one day characterize his presidency.

From their seats at Boston's Fleet Center, the Clintons were impressed, but they never figured the fresh-faced keynoter for real competition. *Nice speech, but let him accomplish something first*, they thought. With Kerry's campaign going down in flames, Hillary silently pondered her own presidential bid four years hence.

Though the country knew virtually nothing about him, Obama's address became his springboard to superstardom. We're living in a reality-show era in which style trumps substance, and delivery beats experience. Hillary Clinton, John McCain, and a host of presidential wannabes could never quite grasp that concept. But Obama got it.

CHAPTER 9

Obama's handlers have always been terrified of reporters poking around in the candidate's life. His friendships with Ayers, Khalidi, and others, if fully examined by the press, would tarnish the campaign's sanitized version of reality. But his long-time association with real estate developer and political fundraiser Antoin "Tony" Rezko could have been politically lethal.

Obama came of age in the grungy swamp of Chicago politics. One of those swamp creatures was the Syrian-born Rezko, a veteran of pay-to-play political powerbrokering. Rezko helped raise some $250,000 for Obama's campaigns over the years, $20,000 of which was his own money.

Hillary Clinton was the first to raise the Rezko association during an exchange with Obama in South Carolina: "I was fighting against [Republican] ideas when you were practicing law and representing your contributor, Rezko, in his slum landlord business in Chicago."

Clinton actually let Obama off easy: she avoided any mention of the shady land deal that had recently been consummated between the Rezkos and Obamas. That's where things get interesting.

In 2005, the Obamas submitted an offer on a stately, ninety-six-year-old Georgian revival home on the South Side. The parcel included a vacant lot adjacent to the home. Without the house, the lot was worthless; accordingly, the seller stipulated that the house and the lot be sold together.

Obama couldn't afford the entire parcel. "It was already a stretch to buy the house," he told the *Chicago Tribune*. In stepped Rezko, who agreed to buy the vacant lot.

When the dust had settled, the Obamas purchased the house for $1.65 million, which was $300,000 below the asking price. Simultaneously, Rezko paid (in his wife's name) $625,000 for the adjacent lot. The real estate specialist who prepared the original appraisal alleged that Rezko grossly overpaid for the empty land.

Why, at the height of the real estate boom, was the Obama's purchase discounted by $300,000? And why would Rezko pay above-market value for vacant land which could only be accessed via the Obama property? This was a year after Obama's big convention speech, and he was obviously going places. Was Rezko attempting to engage in a quid pro quo with the rising star? This appears to be self-explanatory: no Rezko, no house.

The more relevant question is: why would Obama go along with such an unsightly proposition?

"There's no doubt that this was a mistake on my part. 'Boneheaded' would be accurate," offered the candidate, after being gently quizzed over the deal. Fortunately for Obama, neither his opponents nor the media pursued the story. The Rezko connection never gained traction as a campaign issue.

Meanwhile, the longtime Obama benefactor was convicted on sixteen counts of fraud and money laundering (all unrelated to the Obama transaction). Sentencing for Rezko was originally scheduled for October 28, 2008, but was postponed to avoid negative publicity so close to the election.

REZKO WAS ONE WORRY. But for Team Obama, the candidate's church, Chicago's Trinity United Church of Christ, and specifically its pastor, the Rev. Jeremiah Wright, represented the sum of all fears.

According to Obama's autobiographies, Wright was his spiritual mentor. He performed the couple's wedding and baptized their two daughters. Obama named his second book, *The Audacity of Hope,* after a Wright sermon. For twenty years, Obama sat in his church as Wright, dressed in traditional African dashiki robes, unleashed a torrent of anti-white, antimilitary, anti-Semitic, anti-American venom on his congregation.

Wright clearly had a following. Trinity United, 8,500 members strong, remains one of the most influential churches in Chicago. Yet his fiery brand of black liberation theology was enough to send at least one famous congregant scurrying for the doors: Oprah Winfrey left the church in the mid-1990s.

Obama invited his pastor to perform the invocation at his campaign announcement in early 2007. However, on the day of the event, the candidate learned that one of Wright's sermons had found its way into the pages of liberal *Rolling Stone* magazine. The sermon listed ten essential "facts" about the United States—according to Wright. ("Fact number two: racism is how this country was founded and how this country is still run!") Wright closed his racially-charged sermon thusly: "And. And. And! GAWD! Has GOT! To be SICK! OF THIS (expletive)!"

Obama nervously disinvited Wright from his kickoff, though his pastor prayed with the candidate prior to the event.

Perhaps unbeknownst to the Obama camp, videos of Wright's sermons were available for sale through the church. Several of his tirades made their way into cyberspace—yet for a year, the press corps ignored their existence. It wasn't until the following March, in the latter stages of the Democratic primaries, that the Wright controversy finally hit the front pages. Following is a snippet of the reverend's more memorable rants:

"The government gives (black men) the drugs, builds bigger prisons, passes a three-strike law, and then wants us to sing 'God Bless America.' No, no, no, *God damn* America—that's in the Bible for killing innocent people. God damn America for treating our citizens as less than human. God damn America for as long as she acts like she is God and she is supreme."

Following 9/11, Wright suggested that the United States had brought the attacks upon itself: "We bombed Hiroshima, we bombed Nagasaki, and we nuked far more than the thousands in New York and the Pentagon, and we never batted an eye...and now we are indignant, because the stuff we have done overseas is now brought back into our own front yards. America's chickens are coming home to roost!"

On the United States: "[And] they will not only attack you if you try to point out what's going on in white America, the U.S. of KKK–A."

On white people: "It's this world...where white folks' greed runs a world in need."

On HIV/AIDS: "The government lied about inventing the HIV virus as a means of genocide against people of color."

"I don't think my church is particularly controversial," offered Obama.

THE TIMING OF THE WRIGHT controversy was golden. Had the story exploded three months earlier, Obama's candidacy would have crashed in Iowa and other early states. But by March, when the national press grudgingly picked up on the story, he was safely ahead of Clinton in the race for delegates. Conversely, by dispensing with the controversy early enough in the year, Obama was assured that the media wouldn't revisit the issue closer to the general election. There would be no "October surprise" involving Jeremiah Wright.

Had any other candidate claimed membership in Wright's church—much less for two decades—you could have written the obituary on his or her political career. Miraculously, Obama not only weathered the crisis, but the media permitted him to spin the story to his advantage. The Democrat weaseled out of the mess by claiming to have been absent from the church for every one of Wright's more flamboyant sermons.

What a coincidence!

The media lapped up his explanation like hound dogs. Evidently forgetting the *Rolling Stone* article just a year earlier, Obama claimed he was surprised to learn that his longtime friend and pastor was capable of making such outrageous statements. It calls to mind the famous line from *Casablanca*: "I'm shocked—shocked!—to find that gambling is going on in here!"

For his part, Wright reveled in the attention. His antics—including a bizarre performance at the National Press Club in which he mocked his critics and jokingly offered himself as a vice presidential candidate—finally forced Obama to disavow his spiritual adviser and leave Trinity.

His initial efforts at damage control having proved successful, the candidate saw the Wright controversy as an opportunity to cash in politically. It would become the trademark of Obama's presidency: never let a crisis go to waste. And how did he pull it off? With a speech, of course.

From Philadelphia, the cradle of democracy—a strategic and symbolic setting—Obama delivered a grandiose address on race relations (referring to his grandmother as a "typical white person"). Press coverage of the address, entitled "A More Perfect Union," was predictably hyperbolic:

"Senator Barack Obama, who has not faced such tests of character this year, faced one on Tuesday. It is hard to imagine how he could have handled it better," opined the *New York Times*.

"Barack Obama didn't simply touch the touchiest subject in America, he grabbed it and turned it over and examined it from several different angles and made it personal. Just steps from Independence Hall in Philadelphia, he rang the bell hard and well," gushed *Newsweek*.

Matthews called it "a speech worthy of Abraham Lincoln."

Even McCain offered that "it was good for all of America to have heard it." (The Republican nominee refused to touch the Wright and Rezko controversies out of fear of being tagged a racist. Is it any wonder he lost?)

The speech was vintage Obama: platitudinous yet evasive. He centered on the thorny issue of race relations, but dodged the questions about Wright which had forced him to this point. Amidst the hoopla, the relevant questions were never asked:

Why did you wait until you ran for president to renounce your church? If you find Rev. Wright's sermons so offensive, why didn't you follow Oprah and find a new house of worship years ago?

You said you weren't aware of your pastor's controversial statements—yet you quoted some of them in your autobiography. How do you explain this?

If you missed each of Rev. Wright's more combative sermons, does that mean you weren't attending church very often?

Did you stay at Trinity because you actually agree with some aspects of black liberation theology?

Your pastor implied that 9/11 was punishment for our nation's sins. Do you believe that the United States' foreign policy in any way brought on the terrorist attacks?

Did you join Trinity because it was a base from which to build a political career?

Nevertheless, the pirouette was successful. Obama played the press like a fiddle; he knew reporters salivate over stories about race. In their euphoria over his speech, the media decided that the matter of Jeremiah Wright was closed. The slate was clean. Those twenty years Obama spent sitting in his pews were wiped from existence.

In the short run, Obama paid a small political price for the controversy. During the latter stages of his titanic battle with Clinton, he was bested in state after state, including Pennsylvania, Ohio, and Texas. Clinton argued that her rival was unable to close the deal with voters. However, unluckily for her, the Wright story hit about a month too late to save her candidacy.

OBAMA'S ARROGANCE NEARLY DID him in during the Pennsylvania primary. Watching him bowl a thirty-seven was amusing ("what a nerd," said one of my students), but his deeper feelings about small-town Americans weren't nearly as funny.

Trailing ahead of the Keystone State's April primary, Obama attended a fundraiser in San Francisco, which is about as far from the heartland as one can get, geographically and culturally. One of the wealthy liberals in attendance asked the candidate why many Middle Americans remained stubbornly impervious to his charms. It was a question which cried out for humility and restraint, but Obama is willfully incapable of eating humble pie.

Not realizing his remarks were being recorded (which is foolish in itself), Obama dished out a scolding to the American heartland: "They get bitter, they cling to guns, or religion, or antipathy to people who aren't like them, or anti-immigrant sentiment, or antitrade sentiment, as a way to explain their frustrations."

His answer may have set a record for the most insults squeezed into a single sentence.

But the armchair philosopher wasn't through. Those small-town Americans will invariably blame the messenger, he opined: "And when it's delivered by a forty-six-year-old black man named Barack Obama, that adds another layer of skepticism." His rich donors yukked it up in the background. (They might have expected him to throw in a few redneck jokes for good measure.)

Those words testify to the influences of Ann Dunham, Frank Davis, Jeremiah Wright, the Marxist professors, and so many other leftists who have helped shape Obama's worldview since his childhood. He might go down in history as the first man to seek the presidency whilst openly scorning his countrymen.

The remarks were first exposed by Mayhill Fowler, an Obama supporter who attended the fundraiser and recorded the candidate. Alarmed by what she heard, Ms. Fowler posted the comments on *The Huffington Post,* a left-wing website on which you wouldn't expect to find this type of dirty laundry.

"What Barack Obama's remarks last night in San Francisco reveal is his self-confidence—to the point of cockiness—right now," she wrote. Subsequent to the incident, Fowler was harassed and even received death threats from Obama backers.

The remarks came to be known as "Bittergate" or alternately, "God and guns."

Said Clinton in response: "Pennsylvanians don't need a president who looks down on them…I don't think it helps to divide our country into one America that is enlightened, and one that is not." (Of course, Clinton's comments smack of hypocrisy. No one can forget her crack in 1992 about "staying home and baking cookies"—an obvious swipe at stay-at-home mothers.)

Obama never apologized (apparently, he only apologizes for his country); he merely regretted the "wrong choice of words." Perhaps owing to the lack of religiosity in his own life, Obama was guilty of stereotyping people of faith. He fails to realize that people are religious *not* because they are angry at their government—an absurd argument on its face—but rather because they hold a deep and abiding faith in God. Obama is unable and unwilling to recognize that those Judeo-Christian principles built this country and made it great. Instead of embracing those values, he scorns them.

The Wright association and the God-and-guns controversy formed a one-two punch that should have knocked Obama out of presidential contention for good. Any other candidate wouldn't have sniffed the same area code as the White House. But once more, the timing was fortuitous. Obama was trounced in the Pennsylvania primary, but by then he'd all but clinched the Democratic nomination.

The episode illustrates, beyond any doubt, that Obama doesn't share the same values as most Americans, not the least of which is their love of God and country. Partisans defend Obama as incorrigibly sophisticated. To the rest of us, he's simply arrogant and clueless. One wonders how often he's expressed his contempt for the heart and soul of his country without getting caught.

CHAPTER 10

PRIOR TO WORLD WAR II, Argentina was one of the wealthiest countries in the hemisphere. Under the guise of eliminating poverty, President Juan Perón nationalized large sectors of the economy and ran up a massive debt which could never be paid down.

Perón and his charismatic wife, Evita, rose to power through demagoguery and deceit. The pair borrowed and spent the nation into economic ruin; half a century later, Argentina retains only a shadow of its former greatness. Once thriving and prosperous, today the nation is little more than a banana republic.

As Britain's Margaret Thatcher put it, sooner or later, you run out of other people's money to spend.

Fiscal responsibility may not be fun or popular or cool—just ask McCain how that message played politically—but Argentina's plight could well be ours. It may be that we have our own version of Juan and Evita Perón occupying the White House today.

The United States Department of the Treasury estimates that if Obama's debt-funded spending spree continues unabated, servicing the federal debt will reach an incredible 102 percent of gross domestic product (GDP) by the year 2015. That means that our debt will exceed the nation's economic activity, and soon. Obama is pursuing the same unsustainable borrow-and-spend policies that decimated the economies of Greece, Argentina, and other second- and third-world nations. The difference is that Obama is actually moving faster.

IS THIS PRESIDENT A SOCIALIST? At the risk of sounding Clintonian, the answer may depend on your definition of socialism.

Obama has proceeded at breakneck speed in his quest to reshape the nation, using European-style socialism as his economic model. He does so in spite of all empirical evidence that the big-government approach has failed everywhere. In fact, history has demonstrated that the larger the government, the greater the misery and eventual downfall of a nation. The Soviet Union was an extreme example, but this phenomenon is evidenced by failed socialist models throughout Europe and our own hemisphere.

In socialist states, government strangles efficiency. The private sector is forced to subsidize massive, unproductive bureaucracies; these public-sector jobs, in turn, create nothing of value. For this reason, most European nations suffer chronically high unemployment rates. The United States surpassed our European cousins in terms of economic productivity decades ago for precisely this reason. We've unleashed the power of free markets, innovation, and entrepreneurship, while keeping government limited in its size and scope. Our emphasis has been on the creation of private-sector jobs—positions which actually create wealth and contribute to prosperity.

This maxim holds even *within* a nation: high-tax bastions such as California and New York continue hemorrhaging jobs to pro-business strongholds like Texas.

Western Europe was a hotbed of economic productivity until the blight of socialism overtook the continent. Nowhere is this more evident than in Greece, the birthplace of Western culture, where cradle-to-grave socialism drove the nation's debt to an unsustainable 115 percent of GDP. The eurozone's other fifteen members were forced to rescue Greece's embattled economy to prevent a continentwide financial meltdown.

How did this happen to Europe, and how is Obama effecting a similar outcome in the United States?

The answer is found in an old adage attributed to French scholar and historian Alexis de Tocqueville: "[A democracy] can only exist until the majority discovers it can vote itself largess out of the public treasury. After that, *the majority always votes for the candidate promising the most benefits.*"

Once politicians realize they can bribe the voters with other people's money, they'll promise more of it; many elections thus come down to which candidate can outpromise the other. Perhaps it's human nature. Once a country starts down that road, it's almost impossible to turn back.

De Tocqueville's prophecy contains a chilly admonition to future generations: loose fiscal policy, he wrote, is "always to be followed by a dictatorship, then a monarchy."

SO MANY EUROPEANS HAVE come to depend on the government, via public-sector jobs or social-welfare benefits, that the system can never be changed through the electoral process. After all, who would ever vote to cancel their own check? Big government has bred a culture of dependence, which in turn deprives citizens of their economic liberty. It is an inherently self-fulfilling enterprise.

European workers who hold productive, private-sector jobs abhor their socialist regimes, but they are powerless to stop it. Those on the

receiving end of government largesse, along with their political sympa-
thizers, comprise a voting bloc which is large enough to maintain the
status quo in perpetuity.

In the United States, the "receivers" have historically lacked the
votes to impose a permanent socialist realignment upon the nation.
This has differentiated us from our global competitors, to our advantage. While European economies have buckled under the weight of big
government, the United States has enjoyed greater investment and economic growth. That goes a long way toward explaining why we enjoy a
higher standard of living and are the envy of the world.

However, Obama aims to change this, and the so-called "Great
Recession" gave him just the opening he needed. His goal is to vest primary responsibility for economic policy and planning in an all-powerful
central government.

Does big-government socialism create a net drag on the economy?
You bet it does—but rarely do liberals think through the long-term consequences of their policies. In Obama's case, he may not even care.
To him, it's all about "fairness" and power. By swelling the ranks of
the receivers—those who live on the government dole in some form
or fashion—Obama is creating a voting bloc forever obliged to the re-
election of leftist Democrats.

The more the United States resembles a European-style socialist
reverie, the more our economy will regress to their depths. Many of our
competitors across the Atlantic see that as leveling the playing field. Is it
any wonder that international socialists so heartily embraced the Obama
candidacy?

Next time you encounter an Obama supporter—if you can find anyone who will admit to it—see if they work for, or depend on, the government in some way. If so, that explains their allegiance. There won't
be any converting them; that's like taking the food out of their mouths.

Obama would have never been elected if not for those millions of voters whose livelihoods depend on government openhandedness. Social-welfare recipients and government employees (with certain exceptions, such as the military) provide the Democrats a built-in advantage in every election cycle. In fact, public employee unions at the city, county, state, and federal levels actively raise money and organize on behalf of Democratic candidates. Only for those public-sector jobs does organized labor remain a political force. Currently, 52 percent of union members in the United States work for the government.

Within weeks of taking office, Obama rewarded the loyalty of organized labor with two boondoggles of herculean proportions. The first was the taxpayer bailout of General Motors and Chrysler, which arguably saved the United Auto Workers from extinction. The second was the American Recovery and Reinvestment Act of 2009—a.k.a. the "stimulus" bill.

The former prompted Socialist President Hugo Chávez of Venezuela to joke that he and his fellow thug, Cuba's Fidel Castro, might actually be more conservative than Obama. Mocked Chávez on a live broadcast: "Hey, Obama has just nationalized nothing more and nothing less than General Motors. Comrade Obama! Fidel, careful, or we are going to end up to his right!"

Back to our original question: Is Barack Obama a socialist? The answer is yes, very much so. And there are many who like it that way.

"NEVER LET A CRISIS go to waste," preached Rahm Emanuel, Obama's conniving chief of staff. Using the recession as a pretext, the president was free to remake the U.S. economy in a way not seen since the New Deal. The nation's transformation began with an unprecedented spending binge; so fast was the president moving that Congress had little idea what it was funding.

Once elected, Obama spoke at every opportunity about "the worst economy since the Great Depression." He recited it so incessantly that some economists blamed him for making the situation worse. Even his fans in the media grew weary. Obama, however, had a plan: by talking down the economy and placing the blame with his predecessor, he was building the case for his own far-reaching agenda. It was a page out of Alinsky's book.

So, was the recession all Bush's fault, as Obama claims?

During the Bush years, regulators did little to preclude the sale of mortgages to unqualified homebuyers. The Securities and Exchange Commission (SEC) missed warning signs about Bernard Madoff's massive Ponzi scheme. Federal authorities failed to police credit default swaps (betting on other people going bust) and mortgage-backed securities (bonds financed by risky home mortgage payments); the latter's collapse was a major contributor to the financial meltdown.

On the flip side, most of those rules were relaxed well before Bush came into office. With bipartisan congressional support, Clinton deregulated the activities of commercial lenders like Citigroup. Home ownership for minority borrowers was a major policy objective of the Clinton administration; toward that end, regulators pressured mortgage providers to lower their underwriting standards. As a result, many homebuyers obtained mortgages with no money down, and with no verifiable income or assets. Republican calls to reform Fannie Mae, which assisted low-income borrowers by buying up those risky loans, were resisted by Democrats.

It's easy to forget that Bush presided over fifty-two consecutive months of job creation. From August 2003 through December 2007, the U.S. economy grew every month—the longest continuous run on record. Bush's tonic was two rounds of tax cuts (in 2001 and 2003) for every American who paid taxes; he also removed millions of low-income Americans from the federal tax rolls entirely. Those tax cuts provided a bulwark against the economic damage wrought by 9/11.

Bush and Clinton each presided over extended periods of growth, and they each left office with the economy in the throes of recession. There's blame aplenty to go around, from politicians of both parties, to government regulators, to homebuyers who took out mortgages they knew they couldn't afford. But if Obama truly wants to play the blame game, the real villains were greedy, unscrupulous Wall Street bankers—the beneficiaries of taxpayer bailouts.

CHAPTER 11

WHEN BUSH SIGNED THE TARP (Troubled Asset Relief Program) legislation, a $700 billion bailout of the financial services industry, during the final months of his presidency, he all but handed the election to Obama. Restless voters, already leery of unrestrained federal spending, utterly loathed the "too-big-to-fail" mentality. Ironically, Obama, a supporter of the bailout, was the beneficiary of voters' wrath.

Bush was not a spending hawk by any means; his inattention to mounting deficits drove his conservative base bananas. The incoming president would rewrite the book on deficit spending, however. If Bush was playing around with matches, Obama came into office with a blowtorch.

Blaming Bush remained a crutch for Obama, even well into the second year of his presidency. "We inherited a mess," was his enduring mantra. Indeed, Obama inherited a situation which was as bad as any since the Carter era—but on his watch, the economy plunged to depths not seen since the Great Depression.

Eventually Obama was forced to take ownership of the economy; the Democrat had, after all, campaigned as the doctor with the cure. Yet it was clear from the start that he was practicing medicine without a license. Obama's "cures" only made the patient sicker. The first of those fixes was the mammoth $862 billion stimulus bill.

The stimulus was championed as a tourniquet necessary to stop the bleeding. It was critical to pass the plan immediately, the administration warned—even before members of Congress had a chance to read it—lest the economy plunge even deeper into recession. The stimulus passed with lightning speed. Once the dust had settled, it was left to an army of accountants to figure out exactly what Congress had funded.

The package cleared the House of Representatives with no Republican support. Amidst hefty arm-twisting, bribery, and other assorted chicanery, the stimulus barely overcame a Senate filibuster. Only three Republican senators—Susan Collins and Olympia Snowe of Maine, and Arlen Specter of Pennsylvania—voted "yea." (Specter would switch parties within weeks.)

Obama, the renowned postpartisan, thus achieved his first legislative victory on an aggressive party-line vote. Jamming the 1,079-page behemoth through Congress within a matter of hours violated the president's promises of transparency. So much for posting important legislation online first, as he'd pledged repeatedly on the campaign trail.

The Obama plan was actually the second round of stimulus spending; Bush enacted a more modest $168 billion package the previous year. Though the first stimulus had had no discernible impact on the economy, the incoming president forged ahead, undeterred. Obama hoped that flooding the economy with borrowed money would somehow jump-start a recovery. It didn't work.

When Obama took office in January 2009, the national unemployment rate was 7.6 percent. The administration promised that the stimulus would keep it from rising above 8 percent, hence the urgency. Soon thereafter, unemployment officially topped 10 percent. Factoring in the underemployed and those who'd simply given up looking for work, actual unemployment hovered around 20 percent, according to many economists. The employment picture remains alarmingly bleak for the foreseeable future.

In defense of the stimulus, the White House propaganda machine concocted phony numbers and jobs in congressional districts that don't exist. Maybe Biden was right when he offered that "everyone guessed wrong" on the impact of the stimulus. That's one expensive oops.

Conservative economists maintained that a stimulus in the range of $300 billion to $400 billion, centered on payroll tax cuts rather than spending increases, would spark long-range recovery. But then, Obama wouldn't be able to throw around borrowed money like it was candy.

The $862 billion package was a grab-bag of goodies for every liberal special-interest group, principally Obama's public-sector union allies. The stimulus did virtually nothing for the private sector (the few jobs "saved or created" were a terrible return on the investment) but thousands of new federal positions were created. More than $150 billion went to state and local governments to avoid layoffs and rescue a key Democratic constituency.

Bear in mind that with extremely generous benefits packages, every government job is a considerable burden on taxpayers. Federal employees now earn an average salary of over $71,000, compared to $40,000 in the private sector. Many government employees are enjoying exorbitant, recession-proof salaries on the backs of the taxpayers, to the detriment of the economy. Whereas public service was once considered a sacrifice, it now allows for a lush standard of living.

The stimulus came with more strings than a puppet show. To be eligible for funds, states were forced to agree to "maintenance of effort" guidelines, meaning they cannot reduce Medicaid eligibility or cut spending below federally mandated minimums (some Republican governors, wary of the mandates, turned down stimulus money). This imposed a hardship on states in the midst of the recession; some were forced to raise taxes to maintain their eligibility.

The stimulus may not have helped the economy as a whole, but Obama's union allies have to be pleased with the outcome.

DAVE RAMSEY, RENOWNED AUTHOR and financial guru, has a simple catchphrase: "Debt is dumb." A debtor is forced to live within his means, tighten his belt, and, as Ramsey might say, "organize and prioritize." The last thing he does is run up new credit card balances on top of the old.

That is the enduring legacy of the stimulus. Obama plunged us ever deeper into debt, without taking the time to reprioritize our spending.

Every penny of the stimulus was borrowed money, much of it from China and nations that aren't exactly in love with the United States. McCain branded the stimulus "generational theft"; it is our children and grandchildren who will ultimately pick up the tab for Washington's gluttonous spending. That Obama carried the youth vote by such a wide margin (better than two-to-one over McCain) is all the more astonishing. Would even the most naïve college student have voted for Obama, had he or she foreseen the mountain of debt he'd be leaving behind?

New Hampshire Senator Judd Gregg said the administration's spending "basically will bankrupt our children and our children's children." That's what those leftist teachers and professors forgot to mention while they were brainwashing the current generation.

The numbers are truly staggering. Never before have terms like "billions" and "trillions"—incomprehensible sums to the average American—been tossed around with such ease. With interest, the stimulus may end up costing taxpayers some $1.5 trillion over its lifetime.

McCain and Senator Tom Coburn of Oklahoma compiled a list of the most wasteful stimulus projects. Following are just a few of their findings:

- $62 million to build an underground tunnel connecting Pittsburgh's professional baseball and football stadiums to a casino.
- $40 million to upgrade office space and indoor parking for Kansas politicians.
- $200,000 to help indigenous Siberian communities lobby Russian policymakers.
- $500,000 to study the impact of local populations on the Nepalese Himalayas.
- $550,000 to replace windows at a vacant Mount Saint Helens visitors center. (The government has no plans to reopen it.)
- $760,000 to the University of North Carolina at Charlotte to develop a computerized dance program.
- $26 million to a New York City public relations firm to promote the Obama administration's push for health information technology systems.
- $700,000 to researchers at Northwestern University to develop "machine-generated humor."
- $450,000 to study global circulation on Neptune.
- $340,000 to plant palm trees in Fresno, California.
- $1 million for bus station art in Los Angeles.
- $360,000 to the National Institute of Health to promote the impact of its stimulus spending.
- $760,000 for a Georgia Tech assistant professor to study improvised music.
- $700,000 to Georgia State University to study why monkeys respond negatively to iniquity and unfairness.
- $200,000 to researchers in Texas to study people's perception of the stimulus.
- $20 million on signage touting construction projects paid for by the stimulus.

THE STIMULUS WAS JUST the beginning of the red ink. Shortly thereafter, the president signed a $410 billion omnibus spending bill which contained an incredible total of nine thousand earmarks. Before the election, Obama vowed to end wasteful congressional earmarks (a.k.a. pork). Just another campaign promise, broken and forgotten.

"This debt is like a cancer," acknowledged Erskine Bowles, the chief of staff under President Clinton. "It is truly going to destroy the country from within."

It might sound like a Yogi Berra-ism, but it was Biden who declared, "We have to go spend money to keep from going bankrupt." Actually, Yogi was never so moonstruck. One wonders if Obama and Biden have even the most basic understanding of economic principles.

Federal Reserve Chairman Ben Bernanke warned that the United States is following in Greece's footsteps. Obama responded by asking Congress for another $50 billion in social spending.

As a candidate, Obama pledged to pore over the budget page by page, surgically excising the fat and waste. More empty rhetoric. Forget the surgery: Obama is creating a monster. According to numbers from the nonpartisan Congressional Budget Office (CBO), the cumulative national debt—our credit card balance, so to speak—was $5.8 trillion in 2008 when Bush left office. That figure is projected to rise to $11.8 trillion by 2013 and to $17.3 trillion by 2019.

Should those projections hold, he will have doubled the federal debt within five years, and tripled it within ten. Thus, the U.S. government will have accumulated more debt under Obama than under every president in American history—from George Washington to George W. Bush, combined. That's an ugly legacy. And Obama has the temerity to call this a "new era of responsibility."

When government acts like it's playing with Monopoly money, the inevitable consequence is a wholesale devaluing of the currency, à la Argentina and the Weimar Republic. The Federal Reserve is printing money at an alarming pace to buy Treasury debt. Credible economists forecast double-digit inflation as the outcome of such loose monetary policy. Hyperinflation can occur overnight. That would devastate senior citizens and low-income earners while ravaging the values of individual savings and retirement accounts.

As long as there are trees and ink, the Fed can keep printing money as long as it wants. It's a government-run Ponzi scheme. Were this the private sector, those responsible would be sharing a cell with Bernie Madoff.

The only cure for an inflationary cycle is another recession. This is the price we'll pay for runaway spending; this is what happens when your financial house isn't in order. Obama's policies could diminish the standard of living in the United States for generations to come. The Founding Fathers wouldn't recognize the wreckage of the great country they left behind.

CHAPTER 12

PRESIDENT RONALD REAGAN BELIEVED individual Americans know how to spend their money better than nameless, faceless federal bureaucrats. "A rising tide lifts all boats" is the canon of Reagan and other supply-siders. Obama takes the opposite tack: his emphasis isn't on economic growth, but on redistribution of wealth.

Reaganomics sowed the seeds of prosperity for more than two decades. With the exceptions of brief recessions in the early 1990s (which cost the first President Bush his re-election bid) and in 2000-2001 (Clinton's final year in office), the nation enjoyed nearly a quarter-century of robust economic growth. Reagan's policies proved the maxim that when government gets out of the way, the economy is free to reach unlimited heights. "The government which governs least, governs best," he was fond of saying.

The upshot of supply-side economics is evident in any financial transaction. When a business lowers its prices, customers purchase more; likewise, when government lowers taxes, consumers have more to spend in the marketplace. The private sector is the true birthplace of jobs and innovation. Government, on the other hand, is a parasite. It is an inherently nonproductive entity that only drains the economy.

Obama believes government is the solution. He is painfully ignorant of economics and history. To wit: in the 1990s, Congress lowered the capital gains tax rate from 28 percent to 20 percent. Bush further lowered it to 15 percent. Each reduction was followed by a surge of economic activity. In an exchange with ABC's Charlie Gibson, Obama acknowledged as much, but in his next breath insisted he'd "consider raising the capital gains tax *for purposes of fairness.*" In other words, punishing the investor class is more important than fostering economic growth. This is the cornerstone of socialism.

Obama is intent on eviscerating Reaganomics and replacing it with a permanent era of big government. It calls to mind his brazen response to Joe the Plumber, a real entrepreneur, while campaigning in Ohio: "*We have to spread the wealth around.*" This, remember, comes from a man who's never run a business, never made a payroll, and never turned a profit.

Obama would do well to heed the words of Churchill: "Socialism is the philosophy of failure, the creed of ignorance, and the gospel of envy."

AT FIRST GLANCE, THE JOBS report for May 2010 looked sensational. According to the Bureau of Labor Statistics, over 430,000 new jobs were created for the month. Obama trumpeted the report as evidence that his policies were finally working—until it was revealed that nearly all the new hires were temporary census workers.

Private-sector hiring ground nearly to a halt. The May numbers weren't even sufficient to keep pace with normal population growth. The average length of unemployment reached a record thirty-four weeks. Many new private-sector jobs are from temporary employment services. The median wage continues to drop. Youth unemployment hit a record high. The only reason the official statistics aren't worse is that millions of Americans have given up looking for work.

History shows that recessions will reverse themselves within a matter of months, provided the government resists the temptation to meddle. That's the rub.

The United States experienced ten recessions from the end of World War II to 9/11. The average duration was just under a year. This includes the nasty recessions of 1973-1975 and 1981-1982, each of which endured for sixteen months. By the fall of 2010, according to many economists, the Great Recession was in its thirty-first month and counting—triple the length of the postwar average. What happened?

Answer: Obama's policies torpedoed any hope of a lasting recovery. The administration used the crisis to further its own ideological purposes, embarking upon a record-shattering spending spree which the nation could ill afford. Obama relied on the discredited Keynesian theory that massive government borrowing and spending can stimulate long-term economic recovery, rather than embracing classic free-market Reaganomics.

The business community loathes the hyperactivity of this administration on all matters economic. *What'll they think of next?* wonder nervous employers. *Slow down already,* pleads the beleaguered private sector. Obama's health care mandates have disincentivized businesses from taking on additional employees. Will two more job killers on the president's agenda, cap-and-trade (the largest energy tax in history) and card check (de facto forced unionization), eventually become law?

Taxes on American businesses are already the highest in the world, higher than France, Russia, China, or any of our global competitors. Will Obama follow through on his threat to raise them higher? What other sectors of the economy will he attempt to nationalize? And what will Washington's crushing mountain of debt do to interest rates, credit markets, and consumer spending?

Small businesses are the backbone of the economy, but it's impossibly burdensome to open or expand a business in this environment. Ruinous mandates from Washington, a chokehold on financing, the specter of a prolonged recession (or a double-dip recession, as some economists describe it), and the expiration of the Bush tax cuts have everyone worried.

The media have spun the Bush tax cuts as singularly benefiting the wealthy, when in reality they reduced rates for every American who pays taxes. Allowing them to expire, as Obama plans, would create a drag on the economy of 1.1 percent to 1.5 percent, according to analysts at Deutsche Bank. Should upper-income earners curtail their spending, the economy would lurch even deeper into recession.

We have a president who doesn't understand economics, doesn't inspire confidence, and seemingly has a grudge against entrepreneurship. He is unable to accept the fundamental precept that only private enterprise can create real jobs.

It was free-market capitalism—Adam Smith's "invisible hand" principle—that transformed the United States into an economic juggernaut, the likes of which the world has never seen. When government governs least, the engines of innovation and creativity roar the loudest. Recessions, though inevitable, are less painful. The nation prospers and her people thrive.

By design or not, a poor economy turns the people against capitalism. The more we turn, the more we acquiesce to the big hand of government. Is Obama leading the sheep to slaughter?

AS THE REST OF THE world moves toward fiscal restraint, Obama is increasingly becoming an outlier. At the G-20 conference in Toronto, his call for even greater stimulus spending caused a rift with European leaders, who agreed to cut their deficits in half within three years.

In fiscal year 2010, the U.S. government borrowed *40 percent* of the money it spent. At some point, probably sooner than we realize, this massive debt load will destabilize the very foundations of our economy. Such recklessness is already threatening the United States' AAA credit rating, according to Moody's.

When do the unbridled spending and the relentless assault on the business sector finally end? When do the adults step in and take charge? Can true fiscal conservatives even be elected anymore, or will voters continue to back candidates who promise the most giveaways?

Liberals used to say, "Just take it out of the defense budget." But defense has already been carved up like a Thanksgiving turkey. There's no meat left on that carcass.

Social Security and Medicare are going bankrupt; not a peep out of Obama on those looming crises. As of now, baby boomers are paying into the system, yet it's still going broke. What happens when they retire? Can the "baby bust" generation foot the bill? It won't be pretty when those ticking time bombs go off.

During the summer of 2010, Obama pushed Congress to appropriate another $34 billion to extend federal unemployment benefits to a record ninety-nine weeks. Republicans preferred to offset the additional spending with budget cuts elsewhere (reducing nonessential government travel and printing, eliminating government bonuses, and selling unneeded federal property), but Democrats said no. The funds were simply added to the national debt. Rather than entertain the Republicans' alternatives, Obama, ever the partisan, simply called them mean-spirited.

"Spend first, ask questions later," is the theme of this presidency. After all, it's easy to campaign as a Democrat: you promise money for nothing, and criticize anyone who insists on accountability. Soon, however, global lenders will force Washington to choose one of two options, neither of which will be politically expedient: make drastic cuts in spending, or find new sources of revenue.

One of the dangers of Obama's spending rampage is that government programs don't just go away once they're in place. Every nook of the federal government affects employees, special-interest groups, and powerful lobbies with a vested interest in preserving the status quo. Members of Congress cross them at their own political peril. This is the predicament in which Europe now finds itself: government is so interwoven into the fabric of society that politicians are afraid to make necessary cuts, even when their economies are on the brink of collapse.

OBAMA'S GOAL ISN'T MERELY to increase federal outlays for a year or two; his objective is a permanent expansion of government into every corner of American life. Now that he's out of money, how will he accomplish this? By forcing his opponents to accept tax increases. And how will he accomplish *that*? By taking a page from the Clintons.

In the 1990s, Bill Clinton scared elderly voters with the threat of draconian cuts to Social Security and Medicare (he knew the threat was wildly exaggerated, but the fear-mongering served his purpose). Look for Obama to do the same, only this time he'll target baby boomers, who are nearing retirement age, along with seniors.

Scaring voters is an effective, albeit sleazy, political tactic. It's also the type of story the media grabs with both hands...but fortunately, we know they can be trusted to report the facts fairly and accurately. (Ha! Just a little gallows humor there!)

Obama hopes to browbeat Congress into accepting a European-style value-added tax (VAT). Already, Paul Volcker, chairman of the President's Economic Recovery Advisory Board, has suggested the United States consider a VAT to bring deficits under control: "If at the end of the day we need to raise taxes, we should raise taxes," he has said.

Liberals have salivated at the prospect of a VAT for decades. A VAT is, in essence, a tax on the value that is *added* at each stage of production of a commodity; as such, it goes above and beyond an ordinary sales tax. These costs are borne by the consumer in the form of higher retail prices. Government can pick and choose which goods are to be taxed, thereby enhancing its control over our lives. Commodities that meet with Obama's approval (environmentally-friendly products, hybrid vehicles, organic rutabaga, etc.) might be taxed at a lower rate, while burgers, soda, gas, and SUVs could be taxed through the roof.

Politicians also love the VAT because they can phase it in and hope consumers don't notice the difference. Yet the VAT can net hundreds of billions more in annual revenue to the federal government, funding Obama's agenda in perpetuity.

Obama hasn't even begun the scare tactics over Social Security or Medicare, and already he's hinted at the idea of a VAT: "I know that there's been a lot of talk around town lately about the value-added tax. That is something that has worked for some countries. It's something that would be novel for the United States."

The VAT is not to be confused with the FairTax, as advocated by many libertarian economists. The FairTax is a proposal which would abolish all federal income and payroll taxes, replacing them with a national retail sales tax. Needless to say, Obama has no intention of abolishing any income taxes.

What did Obama say about raising taxes prior to the election? "Under my plan, no family making less than $250,000 a year will see any form of tax increase. Not your income tax, not your payroll tax, not your capital gains taxes—not any of your taxes."

This president was willing to say anything to be elected. The American people were just as willing to suspend belief. It turns out we were sold a barrel of low-grade snake oil.

CHAPTER 13

Obama loves baseball, the national pastime, and his hometown Chicago White Sox. When the president threw out the first pitch on opening day, he was proudly sporting a ChiSox cap. It was reassuring to know there's something real, something authentic, something truly all-American about him. If nothing else, I felt the president and I had this in common.

And then Bob Costas interviewed him at the 2009 All-Star game. Obama, who's lived in Chicago half his life, referred to the home of his beloved White Sox as "Cominskey Field."

There's no such thing as Cominskey Field. *Comiskey Park* was the home of the Chicago White Sox for nearly a century. This is not an obscure fact. Every baseball fan, and certainly every Chicagoan, knows this.

On opening day of the following season, a broadcaster threw Obama this hardball: "Who was one of your favorite White Sox players growing up?"

Obama hedged awkwardly but couldn't name any: "You know, I, I, thought that, you know, the truth is that a lot of the Cubs I liked too... but...

I did not become a Sox fan until I moved to Chicago... But when I moved to Chicago, I was living close to, what was then Cominskey Park."

Again with "Cominskey." I didn't know whether to laugh or cringe.

This was an example of Obama's ubiquity getting him into trouble. If the man doesn't know the first thing about baseball, what on earth is he doing in a broadcast booth? Why keep pretending? Is the whole thing an act, so we'll think he's a regular guy after all?

Remember when baseball used to be a reprieve from politics?

Here's an idea: if politicians promise to stay away from our sports, we'll refrain from making any "he throws like a girl" jokes.

FROM 2000-2003, THE OBAMAS earned about $250,000 per year. During this period, the couple's charitable giving came out to less than 1 percent of their income, according to their tax returns. Less than 1 percent, from the man who preaches about spreading the wealth around. He must be talking about other people's wealth.

And then there's the Bidens, who gave even less of their income (0.15 percent and 0.31 percent) to charity in 2006 and 2007, respectively. By contrast, Bush routinely donated more than 10 percent, while the reviled Cheney gave as much as 77 percent of his income away.

Like most presidents before them, Bush and even Clinton were faithful churchgoers. Bush was one of the nation's most devout chief executives, and he made frequent reference to the importance of faith in his life. Another deeply religious president was Franklin Roosevelt, who urged Americans to pray and regularly included prayers in his speeches.

The same could not be said for Obama, whose Sunday mornings are usually reserved for the gym or the links. Obama attended church exactly three times during his first year in office.

Bush honored National Prayer Day in each of his eight years in office, inviting Christian and Jewish leaders to the East Room for an interfaith service. Obama abruptly canceled the tradition. Religion obviously isn't a big deal to the forty-fourth president.

TAKING OFFICE DURING AN ERA of terrorism, international unrest, and economic recession would weigh on any incoming commander in chief. At times, Obama has appeared frustrated and overwhelmed. He's become humorless. He's complained about his challenges. It was reported that his hair was graying, and he'd been playing golf to relieve the pressure. (Bush was mocked in the press for spending too much time on the links. Obama had already played more rounds of golf in one year than Bush did in eight.)

To compensate for his lack of experience, Obama selected Biden, the longtime senator from Delaware, as his running mate. Biden is familiar to many Americans as a plagiarizer who was forced to withdraw from the 1988 presidential campaign. During the Democratic primaries that year, he "borrowed" a stump speech from British politician Neil Kinnock without attribution. It was also revealed that he'd received an "F" on account of plagiarism while in law school.

Biden's most cringeworthy moment from the 1988 campaign occurred during an exchange with a voter who inquired about his grades: "What law school did you attend, and where did you place in that class?" asked the voter.

"I think I probably have a much higher IQ than you do," thundered Biden, jabbing his finger angrily. It was an unpresidential moment to say the least, but the candidate wasn't finished. Sporting his trademark smirk, Biden rattled off a list of his academic credentials (he was in the top half of his law school class at Syracuse University, and was named the outstanding student in political science at the University of Delaware). When it was revealed that both claims were untrue, the senator was forced to quit the campaign.

In 2006, Biden's motormouth got him into trouble again. This time, it was a bad attempt at a racial joke: "In Delaware, the largest growth in population is Indian-Americans moving from India. You cannot go to a 7-Eleven or a Dunkin' Donuts unless you have a slight Indian accent." Being a liberal Democrat, Biden got a pass from the media.

Like a corpse from the grave, he resurfaced in 2008, his trespasses apparently forgiven and forgotten. Joseph Robinette Biden Jr. might be the first man in history to be forced out of a presidential campaign due to scandal—only to return, years later, on a major-party ticket.

THE OBAMA WHITE HOUSE is stocked with academics, journalists, lawyers, and career politicians. Action-oriented business people are few. The Chicago political machine dominates the president's inner circle, promises of change notwithstanding.

Chicago politics has been characterized by graft, greed, corruption, and intimidation since at least the days of Al Capone. "If they bring a knife to the fight, we bring a gun. That's the Chicago way," boasted Obama.

No one embodies the Chicago style like Emanuel. The president's first chief of staff was widely renowned as a foul-mouthed bully with an abrasive, take-no-prisoners approach. He cut his teeth as a political operative in the Clinton White House and as a member of Congress. Emanuel once mailed a dead fish to a pollster he considered disloyal. For his hard-nosed, ruthless style, he earned the nickname "Rahmbo."

Another veteran of the Chicago machine is Valerie Jarrett, one of the Obamas' oldest and closest friends. Said one Democratic operative: "She knows where are all the bodies have been buried in the past thirty or so years of Chicago politics." Arguably the president's most trusted adviser, the Iranian-born Jarrett was a wealthy slumlord with ties to Rezko. That landed her a spot on Judicial Watch's list of Washington's "Ten Most Wanted Corrupt Politicians" for 2008.

Anita Dunn was another senior adviser, serving as White House communications director for much of 2009. In a speech to high school students, she listed the infamous Mao Zedong as one of her favorite political philosophers. (Mao, the Communist Chinese revolutionary leader, was one of the worst mass murderers of the twentieth century.)

Eric Holder, Obama's choice for Attorney General, celebrated his confirmation by calling the United States "a nation of cowards" on race relations. Welcome to the postracial presidency.

Obama named some three dozen high-ranking officials known as czars to his administration. Unlike most presidential appointees, these individuals are not subject to congressional confirmation and oversight, hence the designation. The czars influence everything from the auto industry to health care to technology to Afghanistan. Their authority is practically absolute. Critics have likened their power to a shadow government.

While czars have been around for decades, no president in history has named so many, so fast. That earned Obama a rebuke from the late Sen. Robert Byrd, who accused the president of attempting to bypass Congress. The West Virginia Democrat complained that the appointments "threaten the constitutional system of checks and balances."

The most notorious of these czars was one Van Jones: activist, environmentalist, civil rights attorney, author, and self-professed communist.

It's hard to know where to begin with Jones. He was an ardent supporter of Mumia Abu-Jamal, a death-row inmate who was convicted of the murder of a Philadelphia police officer. Jones also signed a petition alleging that the Bush administration was complicit in the 9/11 attacks and demanding an investigation. (He'd have a lot to chat about with Rev. Wright.)

During his six-month tenure as "Green Czar," Jones controlled tens of millions of dollars in stimulus funds, virtually without oversight.

Dogged reporting by radio and television commentator Glenn Beck and others finally sent this dangerous radical into exile.

BEFORE THE EMBARRASSING SAGA of Van Jones, the administration had egg on its face for failing to vet other high-profile nominees. Former Senate Democratic Leader Tom Daschle, an early Obama supporter, was appointed secretary of Health and Human Services. It turned out that Daschle "forgot" to report taxable income from 2005-2007.

Although Biden famously preached that paying one's taxes is the patriotic thing to do, that doesn't apply to the rich and powerful (and liberal). The administration stood by its embattled nominee after Daschle paid a whopping $140,000 in back taxes and interest. Thanks largely to pressure from talk radio and conservative blogs, Daschle bowed out.

Treasury secretary nominee Timothy Geithner likewise failed to pay his fair share to Uncle Sam. Obama urged the Senate to ignore the $34,000 oversight; Geithner's wizardry in all matters economic was needed to resolve the financial crisis, we were told. Geithner paid his back taxes and was confirmed as Treasury secretary; the nation soon learned he was no better at managing the economy than he was at mastering TurboTax. This may be the first president in history to have willfully installed a tax cheat as head of the IRS.

Lightning struck a third time when it was revealed that Ron Kirk, Obama's choice for U.S. trade representative, owed nearly $10,000 in back taxes. Of course, he was confirmed.

We're not finished. The husband of Labor secretary nominee Hilda Solis settled fifteen different tax liens against his business just in time for her confirmation.

Not so fortunate was Nancy Killefer, named by Obama as chief performance officer, another newly created position in the ever-growing federal bureaucracy. It turned out that Killefer, a former Treasury

Department employee and IRS Oversight Board member, failed to pay unemployment taxes. She withdrew her nomination.

Obama is rapidly expanding government into every crevice of our lives, yet he's surrounded himself with wealthy advisers who flout the tax man. If any of us laymen had failed to pay our taxes, would the IRS have been as forgiving?

Jay Leno joked that with so many Obama nominees settling up their tax bills, the new president had found a way to pay off the national debt.

Taxpayers weren't laughing at the mess delivered by the political neophyte and his Chicago cronies. With so many tax cheats and leftist radicals named to top administration posts, Americans were beginning to wonder whether this gang was corrupt, incompetent, socialist—or all of the above.

CHAPTER 14

GOVERNMENT-RUN HEALTH CARE has been an abject failure everywhere it's been tried. There's not a single instance of it succeeding anywhere on the globe; as with socialism, the big hand of government always, *always* diminishes quality. But the left doesn't want this debate.

Liberals can be insufferable. The United States is the only industrialized nation without universal coverage, they tirelessly remind us. They fail to mention that our health care system is also the envy of the world.

Universal coverage, of course, is code for socialized medicine. The European and Canadian systems are the universal gold standard for socialized care, so it would be helpful to analyze their models before we rush to emulate them. Liberals won't tell you (and may not even realize) that Europeans and Canadians flock to the United States for medical treatment. They're tired of the lines, the waiting lists, the impersonal nature, and the overall poor quality of government-run health care.

The head of a Canadian province, in fact, came to the United States for heart surgery in early 2010. "This was my heart, my choice, and my health," said Newfoundland Premier Danny Williams, who traveled to Miami on his own dime for his procedure. Italian Prime Minister Silvio Berlusconi didn't trust his socialized system either: in 2006, he too journeyed to the United States for heart surgery.

If Obama has his way, when foreign leaders need life-or-death medical procedures, they won't have any place to go. That's because he's intent on dragging our health care system down to their levels.

As a wise commentator put it, do we really want the same government that botched Hurricane Katrina, the Gulf oil spill, and the Enron and Madoff scandals, running our medical care? Do we want every medical appointment to feel like a trip to the DMV or the IRS?

BRITAIN'S DANIEL HANNAN, MEMBER of the European Parliament, warned Americans against going down his country's road. Britain's socialized system has discouraged students from entering the medical profession, and many of his nation's best and brightest physicians have immigrated to the United States.

Those who live under socialized care are more likely to be dissatisfied with their system. Surveys reveal that more than 70 percent of Canadians, Germans, Britons, and Australians believe their systems need "fundamental change" or "complete rebuilding." By contrast, 85 percent of Americans said they were happy with our current health care. We may not think it's perfect, but the vast majority are satisfied. What we're worried about is the government mucking things up.

Canadian and British patients wait about twice as long as we do to see a specialist, to have radiation treatment, or to undergo elective surgeries like hip or knee replacements. Our northern neighbors receive about half as many coronary interventions as we do. Heart patients must often wait months for treatment.

Americans enjoy superior access to preventive cancer screening (mammograms, pap smears, PSA tests, and colonoscopies). We have higher survival rates than Europeans for common cancers. In the United Kingdom, mortality rates for breast and prostate cancer are roughly two and six times higher, respectively, than in the United States.

Americans have access to the latest technological innovations; most medical and pharmaceutical breakthroughs originate in the United States. The entire world benefits from our ingenuity and entrepreneurial spirit. And here's the kicker: despite our sedentary lifestyle and imperfect diet, lower-income and older Americans are in better health than their Canadian counterparts.

Once a nation starts down the road toward socialized medicine, it is extremely difficult to turn back. The U.K. has taken steps to decentralize its publicly-funded National Health Service (NHS). That's no small task: the NHS has become so bloated that it is now the second-largest employer on the planet, behind only the Chinese Red Army.

OBAMA VOWED TO BRING "change" to America—whether we wanted it or not. Despite inheriting a recession and fighting two wars, he chose to focus his first year on "reforming" the nation's health care system. Let's examine his signature domestic priority, the Patient Protection and Affordable Care Act, a.k.a. ObamaCare. The plan will:

- cut $500 billion from Medicare for seniors.
- add thirty million new patients to an already burdened system, without adding new doctors.
- require de facto rationing of health care and drive up premiums for all Americans.
- require the uninsured to purchase health insurance policies, pay a fine, or go to jail.

- tax medical devices such as pacemakers.
- cut reimbursements to doctors who order too many tests.
- add hundreds of billions to the federal deficit.
- exempt the president and members of Congress.
- carve out special exemptions for Democrat-friendly unions.
- curtail health care for older Americans who've paid taxes all their lives, while providing coverage for illegal immigrants who haven't paid a dime.
- force taxpayers to subsidize abortions.
- grant unprecedented powers to political appointees at the Department of Health and Human Services.
- empower government bureaucrats to make many of our health care decisions.
- disincentivize research and development into new drugs and technology.
- impose the largest tax increase in American history—as much as $500 billion, by some estimates. This would hit the middle class as well as high-end earners. Americans for Tax Reform found at least seven tax hikes on individuals making less than $250,000, in violation of Obama's famous pledge.

SANTA CLAUS ISN'T REAL, and this legislation was never really about health care. It was always, at its core, a power grab by Washington; another massive expansion of federal authority. Once government controls basic necessities like health care, the people become its servants. Dictators the world over know this to be true.

ObamaCare is a means to seize more of our freedoms; to control one-sixth of the U.S. economy; to reward special interests; and to make us more "liked" by international socialists, whose health care systems couldn't hold a candle to our own.

Obama began by touting his plan as a means for covering the uninsured. When we learned that the "uninsured" includes millions of illegal immigrants and healthy or self-employed individuals who choose to forgo health insurance, he shifted his emphasis to lowering costs. After the CBO made it clear that the plan would drive the nation deeper into debt, the president started talking about "insurance reform." Each day brought a new rationale.

As the public turned against his scheme, Obama talked up its more "popular" provisions, such as mandatory coverage for individuals with pre-existing conditions. Despite his rhetorical prowess, the plan continued to tank in public-opinion surveys. If this was an audition, Obama was blowing his lines.

The reason for the public opposition is simple. ObamaCare lays the groundwork for socialized medicine; it is the camel's nose under the tent. This, the American people will not abide.

"I happen to be a proponent of a single-payer, universal health care plan," Obama told the AFL-CIO in 2003 ("single-payer" is another synonym for socialized medicine).

ObamaCare makes that goal inevitable. If an individual has a choice between buying private medical insurance and paying a fine, he'll opt for the cheaper alternative every time. If the premium is more expensive, he'll pay the fine, knowing that if he ever gets sick, the insurance companies will be required by law to accept him for coverage. Likewise, businesses will simply drop coverage for their employees if it's cheaper to just pay the fine. (This is already happening under Massachusetts' universal plan: firms are canceling health insurance, forcing their employees into state-subsidized care.)

This places insurance companies in an impossible situation. In most cases, premiums would cost thousands of dollars more than the fines. The result is the gradual death of the private insurance industry. Obama admitted in an interview in 2007 that this was his objective: "But I don't think we're going to be able to eliminate employer coverage immediately... There's going to be, potentially, some transition process. I can envision a decade out, or fifteen years out, or twenty years out."

Once the insurance companies have been eliminated, all Americans will be forced into an expanded Medicare system—the only remaining option. Medicare then reduces payments to doctors; those doctors in turn will be forced into HMOs, which will answer to the government. Most private-care providers will simply cease to exist. The federal government will have de facto control of the health care economy. Uncle Sam will become our daddy.

This is socialized medicine. This is ObamaCare.

THROUGHOUT 2010, POLLS CONSISTENTLY showed the majority of Americans opposed to the Obama takeover of health care. In spite of the media's aggressive cheerleading for the bill, independents were against it two to one. Then there's the intensity gap: respondents who "strongly oppose" the measure outnumbered those who "strongly support" it by the same two-to-one margin.

Only 28 percent of respondents say shifting workers to a government health plan is a good idea, according to Rasmussen Reports. Large majorities in swing congressional districts believe ObamaCare will make them, their loved ones, the economy, and the U.S. health care system worse, not better.

"I don't know how passing health care will play politically, but I do know that it's the right thing to do," blustered Obama.

This president never tires of insulting our intelligence. In his mind, only he knows what's good for the governed. At one point, the president faulted himself for not adequately explaining his proposal to the public.

Such arrogance calls to mind the old quip: I've been wrong only once in my life, and that was when I *thought* I was wrong.

This condescension finally got Obama into hot water politically. Per Rasmussen, his presidential approval index turned from positive to negative in mid-2009, and there it's stayed. By the summer of 2010, the index reached negative twenty-two. It's an extraordinary fall from grace. In the history of polling, no president's approval ratings have fallen so far, so fast. The man who entered office with such enormous good will managed to squander it early in his presidency.

Angry with conservative critics, Obama's team encouraged Americans to snitch on anyone who might oppose his plan. In a post called "Facts Are Stubborn Things," the White House wrote: "There is a lot of disinformation about health insurance reform out there, spanning from control of personal finances to end-of-life care. These rumors often travel just below the surface via chain emails or through casual conversation. Since we can't keep track of all of them here at the White House, we're asking for your help. If you get an e-mail or see something on the web about health insurance reform that seems fishy, send it to flag@whitehouse.gov."

Under pressure, the administration removed the website, which critics called an effort to intimidate opposition and stifle free speech. With tactics like this, is it any wonder Obama's ratings went into a free fall?

CHAPTER 15

O BAMA'S APPETITE FOR GOVERNMENT control of the private sector, including health care, banking, mortgages, student loans, and the automobile industry, is insatiable. That he governs against the will of the people doesn't bother him. Obama has said he'd rather be a one-term president than compromise his agenda.

According to the Gallup Poll, more than twice as many Americans describe themselves as conservative than liberal. It was during the summer of 2009 that the conservative majority finally pushed back. ObamaCare looked like a done deal when members of Congress went home for their August recess. And just like that—*wham!*—the momentum shifted away from the president.

While Obama was riding high, socialized medicine appeared inevitable. The left was on the verge of foisting a massive entitlement program—the kind that never goes away once it's in place—upon the nation over the objections of dispirited conservatives. But in the summer of 2009, the people found their voice. Government-run health care was halted, temporarily, by a once-in-a-generation, grassroots phenomenon: tea parties and town halls.

The Tea Party movement can trace its origins to an emotional on-air commentary by CNBC's Rick Santelli in February. The stimulus bill was signed into law February 17, 2009, and the very next day, Obama announced the Homeowners Affordability and Stability Plan, a $75 billion mortgage bailout. Santelli had had enough. Thus was born the "rant of the year":

"The government is promoting bad behavior! I have an idea…The new administration is big on computers and technology. How about this: why don't you put up a website to have people vote…as a referendum to see if we really want to subsidize the losers' mortgages?"

Santelli was on the floor of the Chicago Board of Trade. When the traders began applauding, he turned from the camera, unscripted, and asked, "This is America! How many of you people want to pay for your neighbor's mortgage, that has an extra bathroom and can't pay their bills?" The response was as expected.

He turned back to the camera and asked, "President Obama, are you listening? We're thinking about having a Chicago tea party in July!"

The clip went viral. Santelli captured the mood of the country. Taxpayers were fed up with the spending, takeovers, and bailouts, starting under Bush and intensifying under Obama. In answer to his question, of course Obama wasn't listening, nor were members of Congress—until Santelli's words proved prophetic. The era of the tea parties was upon us.

Ordinary citizens were outraged by the steady drumbeat of socialism, the erosion of our liberties, and the arrogance of our elected officials. The American people—Republicans, Independents, and even some Democrats—grew genuinely fearful for the future of their country. The Tea Party movement stood for less government and more individualism.

Millions of Americans rallied to send this powerful message to Washington. Events were held across the country on April 15 (tax day), July 4, and September 12 (the day following the anniversary of the 9/11 attacks). While a tin-eared president stayed holed up inside the Beltway, senators and congressmen got an earful from their constituents as they hadn't since the civil rights movement.

Tea partiers got creative with their signs:

"Socialism is trickle-up poverty."

"Stop spending our grandchildren's future."

"The Bolsheviks promised change, too."

"Don't spread my wealth—spread my work ethic."

"Honk if I'm paying your mortgage."

"Annoy a liberal: take personal responsibility."

"Stop the war on prosperity."

"Don't tell Obama what comes after a trillion!"

And the best of all…

"OBAMA: One Big, Awful Mistake, America."

IN THE SPIRIT OF THE FOUNDERS, Americans also packed town hall meetings across the country to deliver their message to their representatives. *Have you even read the health care bill?* the people asked. They hadn't (that would have taken weeks, given its sheer volume). Like the stimulus, many Democrats committed to vote for the 2,700-page plan before they had any idea what was in it.

Members of Congress spent the summer of 2009 sweating and squirming. Some avoided town hall meetings altogether (you know you're having an impact when elected officials start hiding from their own constituents). Obama plowed ahead with his agenda anyway, dismissing the rallies as a stunt by Fox News.

While Fox enjoyed hefty ratings surges whenever it covered the tea parties, competing networks chose to ignore and belittle them. Tea partiers were maligned as bigots and right-wing extremists. Once more, the race card was exploited in lieu of substantive debate.

The "racist" charge usually means the other side has exhausted any intellectual arguments, or perhaps didn't have any to begin with. It's their way of ending the debate and shaming opponents into silence. In today's political climate, charging racism is like crying wolf. The word is so overused and abused that unfortunately, it's lost its impact.

It was a ludicrous allegation anyway. Far from how they are portrayed in the media, tea partiers are a remarkably diverse group: as many as half are self-identified Independents or Democrats. They are the salt of the earth: grandmothers and grandfathers, parents and children, veterans and patriots, all standing against the rise of socialism and the threat of tyranny. The tea partiers are the modern-day civil rights protesters.

With his agenda in jeopardy, the president sought to counterpunch. He turned to key allies such as ACORN, the SEIU, and Organizing for America (an offshoot of the Obama campaign), to do his dirty work. The goon squads were deployed to town hall meetings to intimidate opponents of ObamaCare, many of whom were elderly.

"I want you to argue with them and get in their face!" instructed Obama, borrowing another page from Alinsky. "Punch back twice as hard."

In some cases, union members were admitted early to stack the town halls. In others, SEIU thugs menaced participants as they entered the meetings. At times, violence ensued. At a St. Louis, Missouri town hall, a black conservative named Kenneth Gladney was passing out "Don't Tread On Me" flags when he was assaulted by SEIU members. Gladney was taken to the emergency room to be treated for injuries to his knee, back, elbow, shoulder, and face. Six people were arrested in connection with the attack.

Elsewhere, brawny SEIU members physically blocked entrances to public meetings held by Democratic congressmen. Cameras caught them pushing, bumping, and bullying participants, and even applying a choke-hold to one man in Tampa. Thanks to the new media, however, the Alinsky gambit backfired. YouTube and other video-sharing sites exposed the tactics to the world. The images contradicted Obama's expired message of hope and change.

So effective were the grassroots protests that the Obama agenda stalled, at least temporarily. The president with the need for speed was left cooling his heels.

IT WAS SARAH PALIN who dealt the first major body blow to ObamaCare. In August 2009, she wrote the following on her Facebook page: "The America I know and love is not one in which my parents or my baby with Down Syndrome will have to stand in front of Obama's 'death panel' so his bureaucrats can decide, based on a subjective judgment of their 'level of productivity in society,' whether they are worthy of health care. Such a system is downright evil."

Palin's condemnation resonated with the nation and threatened to mortally wound the president's plan. ObamaCare will indeed ration care to the elderly, infirm, and disabled based on a health-care measuring tool known as Quality Adjusted Life Years (QALY). Even many Democratic supporters who hadn't read the bill were taken aback.

Supporters were in a panic. The media, as deeply in the tank for Obama as ever, scrambled to debunk Palin's critique. The *New York Times*, long a champion of socialized medicine, blurred the lines between objective journalism and editorial commentary, as is its wont. The paper opened a straight news piece thus: "The stubborn yet false rumor that President Obama's health care proposals would create government-sponsored 'death panels' to decide which patients were worthy of living seemed to arise from nowhere..."

On Capitol Hill, embarrassed Democrats denied that the bill contained death panels—but then promised they would be removed before final passage.

The inclusion of QALY should come as no surprise, as this president has never placed a premium of the value of life. In fact, Dr. Ezekiel Emanuel, brother of Obama's chief of staff, was one of the chief architects of the plan, and the inclusion of QALY is largely for his efforts. Dr. Emanuel has spoken in terms of one's value as a person, and how much time and money should be expended to save that life.

Aside from Dr. Emanuel, the number of advisers to this president with ties to eugenics, notably science czar John Holdren, is chilling. (Eugenics is the belief that the human race can be improved by encouraging or discouraging reproduction based on desirable genetic traits.)

ObamaCare is a proverbial mare's nest; Emanuel's involvement raises even more troubling questions. If a government bureaucrat determines that one's life isn't worth saving, what recourse will any of us have? Will the time come when our age, medical history, genetic makeup, or ability to contribute to society determines our access to care? Is euthanasia looming in our nation's future?

These questions are not beyond the pale. Once an all-powerful central government controls the purse strings of health care, we are literally at its mercy. The death panels, incidentally, were never stricken from the bill.

WHY SHOULD ANY OF US trust ObamaCare to look out for our longevity and well-being? Dating to his years as a state legislator, when he staked out an extremist position on the Born Alive Act, Obama has never respected the sanctity of innocent human life.

This may, in fact, be the most pro-death president in history. He even supports partial-birth abortion, a gruesome procedure (since outlawed) in which a baby is delivered feet-first and then stabbed in the back of his or her skull.

Three days after his inauguration, Obama reversed the Mexico City Policy, which prohibited U.S. tax dollars from funding abortions abroad. (He did so by executive order, one of the many times he's acted without congressional approval.) His cabinet and judicial nominees are universally pro-abortion; he is forcing taxpayers to fund stem-cell research involving the destruction of human embryos; and his first budget eliminated all federal funding for abstinence-only education.

Obama's Department of Veterans Affairs released a guide called "Your Life, Your Choices," which promotes euthanasia for elderly or disabled vets. One section of the guide, "What Makes Your Life Worth Living?", asks veterans to evaluate whether they pose an emotional or financial burden on their family. This is heartbreaking stuff.

Despite his pro-choice position, Obama vowed that his health care proposals would not allow for taxpayer funding of abortion. Predictably, this promise was checked at the door. Pro-life groups got an inkling of what was to come when they were shut out of a White House summit on health care, while Planned Parenthood was invited to attend.

Pro-life advocates, some of whom had championed universal health care in the past, became the fiercest critics of ObamaCare. The president shares the left's ambition of abortion on demand. ObamaCare, by providing federal funding for abortion, affords a means toward that end.

CHAPTER 16

SEVENTY PERCENT OF AMERICANS told pollsters the president should put health care aside for the time being and make economic recovery his priority. More than four out of five believed that it was important for any health care reform legislation to have broad-based, bipartisan support, according to an AP-GfK survey in early 2010. More than two-thirds of respondents said Democrats should try to work with Republicans in good faith.

Public opinion, however, would not stand in this president's way.

This was not the first time Congress tried to take over health care. It was Bill Clinton's top domestic priority early in his administration, but Democrats could never overcome the opposition of the majority of Americans. The Clintons' push for "HillaryCare" in 1993 led directly to the Democrats' huge congressional losses a year later.

By 2009, Democrats controlled 60 percent of the House and Senate, a higher number than Clinton ever enjoyed. Whereas Clinton was forced to compromise on major legislation, Obama didn't need a single Republican vote for passage. The regime was thus free to pursue its agenda unfettered.

Obama paid lip service to bipartisanship and consensus building, but the opposition was never seriously consulted. Instead, Republicans were mocked as the "party of no" for standing up to government-run health care and the rest of Obama's far-left agenda. But this time, the American people saw through his rhetoric.

Campaigning came easily to Obama. Governing was another matter. During the election, his chorus of "Yes we can!" whipped exuberant crowds into a frenzy. One year later, those cries turned to "No you don't!" For so shamelessly flouting public opinion, Obama's party would pay, beginning with a pair of key off-year races.

VIRGINIA AND NEW JERSEY held gubernatorial elections in November 2009, affording voters their first chance to weigh in on the president's agenda. Obama courted Virginia aggressively during his presidential bid, and he was rewarded handsomely for his efforts. For the first time since 1964, the Old Dominion cast its electoral votes for a Democratic presidential candidate.

Obama's success inspired talk that Virginia's transformation from a swing state to a lasting Democratic bastion was complete. The state's gubernatorial election was thus, in many ways, a referendum on Obama; a progress report, so to speak. The verdict was harsh.

The people of the commonwealth couldn't vote the president out of office, but they could vote against his proxy, state Senator Creigh Deeds. After eight years of Democratic rule in Richmond, Republican nominee Bob McDonnell trounced Deeds by eighteen points. McDonnell won by the highest margin of any Virginia gubernatorial candidate in forty-eight years. Ouch.

In New Jersey, a state that voted even more heavily for Obama, incumbent Democrat John Corzine lost by a comfortable margin to Republican challenger Chris Christie. Obama campaigned for the free-spending Corzine in the closing days of the campaign, but alas, by then the magic was gone. Christie was a former U.S. attorney known for prosecuting public corruption among both Republicans and Democrats. When he took the stage on election night, his supporters stole Obama's "Yes, we can!" chant.

For one extraordinary evening, the people of Virginia and New Jersey gave voice to every American. Was Obama listening?

Also in the 2009 election, Republicans won control of the Pennsylvania Supreme Court, the Nassau County (Long Island) legislature, and scores of local races. U.S. Representative Parker Griffith of Alabama, a physician and leading opponent of ObamaCare, switched his party affiliation from Democratic to Republican. Only in a special election for a vacant congressional seat in upstate New York, in which the Republican and Conservative Party candidates garnered a combined 52 percent of the vote, did a Democrat prevail.

The White House tried to pin the losses on lackluster campaigns and poor candidates. The blame was placed everywhere but on the president and his policies. Obama appeared to be in complete denial of the election results. In fact, with renewed urgency he stepped up pressure on Congress to advance his health care legislation.

On November 7, 2009, just four days after the Democrats' electoral thumping, the House of Representatives approved ObamaCare by a margin of 220-215. Speaker Nancy Pelosi, fully aware that the measure was politically toxic, permitted as many Democrats as mathematically possible to defect.

Representative Bart Stupak, a pro-life Catholic from Michigan, and a small but influential cadre of pro-life Democrats managed to insert language into the bill which expressly prohibited federal funding of abortion. For conservatives, this was the silver lining in a very dark cloud.

The Senate was next. The upper chamber voted on Christmas Eve, when they figured no one (except us political junkies) would be paying attention. It was neither easy nor pretty. Votes were bought and sold like cheap stocks. In the end, exactly sixty senators—the bare minimum necessary to overcome a filibuster—voted in favor of ObamaCare. Every Democrat voted "yea"; every Republican "nay."

Significantly, the Senate removed the Stupak language from the bill; it was one of the pro-lifers' own allies, Senator Ben Nelson of Nebraska, who sold them out. As the critical sixtieth vote needed for passage, Nelson could have demanded that the language be preserved, but he acquiesced to party leaders.

Still, the final chapter in this long, ugly saga had yet to be written. The House and Senate, having passed separate versions of the legislation, would have to resolve their differences in a conference committee. Obama was still a long way from taking a final victory lap.

DEMOCRATS HAD GOTTEN TO a filibuster-proof majority in the Senate by hook and by crook. Several members coasted to victory in the anti-Republican waves of 2006 and 2008. But merely controlling the body wouldn't suffice; Democratic leaders set their sights on a super-majority of sixty seats. As circumstances would have it, every conceivable break went their way.

In Alaska, Democrat Mark Begich prevailed only because the incumbent Republican, the late Ted Stevens, was convicted on seven felony counts the week before the election (the convictions were later overturned). Begich won by fewer than four thousand votes.

Sen. Arlen Specter of Pennsylvania, a longtime RINO, finally jumped ship and gave Democrats their fifty-ninth seat. (Specter would go on to lose the Democratic primary the following year. It couldn't have happened to a nicer vulture.)

The most shameless outcome was in Minnesota, where Al Franken stole the all-important sixtieth Senate seat by 312 votes. With a large assist from Mark Ritchie, Minnesota's ACORN-endorsed secretary of state, Franken overtook incumbent Republican Norm Coleman in a protracted, months-long recount. "Missing" Franken ballots kept turning up in heavily Democratic precincts; some Franken votes were counted twice; and many Coleman ballots were rejected. The rules of the recount were continually changed to favor Franken, until he had just enough votes to be declared the winner.

With only forty senators, Republicans could no longer sustain a filibuster. The Democrats were mathematically unstoppable, assuming they could keep all their members in line. President Barack Obama, the man who's so rarely heard the word "no" in his life, now had a Senate chock full of yes-men. The nation watched as Democrats used every one of those votes to ram through the president's health care overhaul.

However, on January 19, 2010, voters had a chance to add a forty-first member to the Republican ranks. This time, it would be epic. And it would come from the unlikeliest place on the planet, when deep-blue Massachusetts went Brown.

THE ELECTIONS IN VIRGINIA and New Jersey were merely the opening acts in the national referendum on President Obama. The main event was a political earthquake centered in ultraliberal Massachusetts. A month after the Senate passed ObamaCare with literally no votes to spare, Republican Scott Brown bested Democrat Martha Coakley in a special election to replace the late Senator Edward Kennedy.

Obama campaigned for Coakley, but the voters of Massachusetts handed the president a rebuke that was utterly stunning in its size and scope. The Bay State had voted for Obama by a whopping margin of twenty-six points, making Brown's victory all the more spectacular.

With support from the Tea Party movement, Brown campaigned to be the "forty-first senator"—a reference to the number necessary to stop ObamaCare in the upper house.

Proving that truth is stranger than fiction, socialized medicine was Kennedy's lifelong political dream. His replacement was elected on a platform of stopping it.

Said Brown on election night: "One thing is clear: voters do not want the trillion-dollar health care bill that is being forced on the American people. I will work in the Senate with Democrats and Republicans to reform health care in an open and honest way. No more closed-door meetings or back room deals by an out-of-touch party leadership. No more hiding costs, concealing taxes, collaborating with special interests, and leaving more trillions in debt for our children to pay. In health care, we need to start fresh, work together, and do the job right."

Thus, the nation's political landscape was transformed faster than you can say "Chappaquiddick." Even Massachusetts, the most Democratic state in the nation, sent an unmistakable message to the big spenders in Washington.

Would the president *finally* take the hint?

CHAPTER 17

Elections, unless they're his own, do not faze Obama. When the Democrats lost control of Congress during the 1994 midterms, Bill Clinton adjusted. Ever the political creature, he simply pivoted to the center, particularly on fiscal issues, to better reflect the mood of the nation. That savvy got him re-elected, and also restored a semblance of fiscal sanity to Washington.

Clinton was many things, but he was no fool. Aside from his extra-marital dalliances, his priority in life was political survival; he had no intention of being remembered as a one-term president. Obama, by contrast, clings to a far-left ideological zealotry, even in the wake of political disaster. His unrelenting pursuit of nationalized health care against the will of the people struck many, even in his own camp, as obsessive. Like a monster in a horror movie, ObamaCare refused to die.

Brown arrived in the Senate four weeks too late for the Christmas Eve vote, but his presence was a game-changer nonetheless. With forty-one members, newly-emboldened Senate Republicans could filibuster the House-Senate conference report, effectively killing the legislation.

ObamaCare was on life support. To keep it alive, Democrats would have to resort to parliamentary gimmicks and charades.

In one possible (though highly unusual) scenario, the House could approve the Senate version of the bill exactly as it read, thereby eliminating the need for a conference committee altogether. However, as Speaker Pelosi put it, "Nobody wants to vote for the Senate bill."

Yes, the Senate bill was *that* bad. Its accession to taxpayer-subsidized abortions was a deal-breaker for Stupak and other swing Democrats. The Senate version also included sweetheart deals for certain states, most notably the "Cornhusker Kickback" and the "Louisiana Purchase," designed to win the support of senators from Nebraska and Louisiana, respectively. Senators from Florida, Vermont, and Connecticut also extracted notable concessions. (As a result, Democratic supporters of ObamaCare would be forced to explain why they voted to send their constituents' money to these favored states.)

In reality, the Senate never intended for its Christmas Eve bill to become law. In its haste to adjourn for the holiday (and avoid a major snowstorm bearing down on Washington), the Senate passed a bill that none of its members had read, much less understood. The legislation was little more than a rough draft; they simply assumed the mess would be cleaned up in conference committee, as usual. But Brown's election, which no one saw coming, now rendered that impossible.

Short of negotiating with Republicans, House Democrats had no option but to swallow hard and pass the Senate version. Would nervous rank-and-file members consent to such a brazen scheme?

At this point, the nation desperately needed a president to step up and show leadership. The situation, largely of Obama's own making, was spiraling out of control. Could he dial down the rhetoric, bring both sides together, and build a truly bipartisan consensus? To do so would have soothed a sorely divided nation. Or perhaps it was time to focus everyone's attention on the economy, leaving the more contentious aspects of health care reform for another day?

Perish the thought. For the White House, it was full-speed ahead.

HOPING TO SCORE A PUBLIC relations coup, Obama hosted a bipartisan health care summit in early 2010. Its ostensible purpose was to hear out the Republicans, yet the president allotted them less than a third of the speaking time. When the inequity was brought to his attention, he quipped, "You're right, there is an imbalance...because I'm the president." Half the room laughed.

Obama can be as sarcastic as Don Rickles on a Saturday night. Unlike Bill Clinton, he doesn't lose his temper; instead, Obama reveals his disdain with an icy stare. Republicans saw plenty of that stare throughout the summit.

There's no doubt the president planned to use the summit as a photo op, with Republicans as little more than stage props. But the GOP came prepared. Republicans presented their case artfully, catching the moderator-in-chief by surprise, and appearing to get under his skin.

McCain pointed out that the health care legislation, like the stimulus, was being rammed through Congress without any collaboration with Republicans: "Both of us during the campaign promised change in Washington. In fact, eight times you said that negotiations on health care reform would be broadcast on C-SPAN...Unfortunately, this product...was produced behind closed doors."

The old war hero was shown no quarter. "Look, let me just make this point, John, because we are not campaigning anymore. The election's over," parried Obama.

Republicans made it clear that they support health care reform—but they implored the president to scrap this bill, start over, and get it right. Senator Coburn, a physician, proposed cracking down on fraud and waste in programs such as Medicaid by having investigators disguise themselves as patients. He pointed to studies which show as much as 20 percent of the cost of federal health care is fraud.

Wyoming Senator John Barrasso, another M.D., floated the idea of expanded health savings accounts. These would allow younger, healthier individuals to opt for catastrophic coverage today, while putting money aside tax-free to cover high deductibles down the road.

Representative Marsha Blackburn of Tennessee championed the right to purchase health insurance across state lines. Such an approach would increase choice and competition, making insurance more affordable, accessible, and accountable. Republicans also advocated allowing small businesses to pool their resources to provide coverage through association health plans.

Wisconsin Representative Paul Ryan denounced the price tag and fiscal chicanery used by the White House to sell the package. The CBO projects that the plan will add more than a trillion dollars in further public debt; the administration used accounting gimmickry to claim a *savings* of $140 billion. That's a huge difference. (Obama offered no credible rebuttal to Ryan—just that icy stare.)

Republicans also made their case for curbing lawsuit abuse, a.k.a. tort reform. Medical malpractice lawsuits, and the mere threat of litigation, are a primary culprit in the rising cost of health care. Approximately 25 percent of doctor referrals, tests, and procedures, and an estimated 13 percent of hospitalizations, are ordered for no reasons other than lawsuit avoidance. Ambulance-chasing trial lawyers have forced doctors to practice costly defensive medicine, and they've put many hospitals and private-care providers out of business.

The CBO estimates that even modest changes would reap substantial savings for the health care consumer. A $250,000 cap on punitive damages, along with a $500,000 cap on damages for pain and suffering, would save the nation $54 billion over ten years. "Loser-pays" rules would also keep junk lawsuits from clogging up the court system.

States with favorable tort climates enjoy greater physician access and lower costs. After Texas passed a comprehensive package of tort reforms in 2003, which capped payouts in malpractice cases, the state was flooded with applications for new medical licenses. Many of the doctors were fleeing "judicial hellholes" like New Jersey and New York City.

Tort reform enjoys popular support. Between 70 and 80 percent of Americans believe the nation suffers from lawsuit abuse. But the powers that be aren't about to bite the hand that feeds them. Attorneys and law firms donated over $178 million to Democratic candidates in the 2008 election cycle alone, including an astounding $43 million to the Obama campaign. No other industry ponied up as much campaign cash to the president.

Tort reform was a no-go from the get-go. The doctors were ignored. Trial lawyers and bureaucrats essentially wrote this legislation.

WITH TIRESOME PREDICTABILITY, Obama rejected each and every Republican recommendation. He had no intention of considering their proposals; ObamaCare, after all, was never truly about improving health care or lowering costs. The summit was a stunt; his pleas for bipartisanship a sham.

Forget the grandiloquence of the campaign; Obama proved himself an ideologue to the core. Having mocked and then ignored the Republicans, he managed to unite the entire caucus against him—no small feat. Even liberal Republicans Snowe and Collins, who voted for the president's stimulus bill a year earlier, couldn't bring themselves to support this disaster in the making.

Nonetheless, the health care summit was the GOP's day to shine. Republicans showed they are much more than the "party of no." (For the record, there's no shame in saying "no" to a radical, leftist agenda. In fact, *stopping* bad legislation is often more important than passing your own.)

Many conservatives and independents had lost faith in the Republicans, and with good reason. The party drifted from its conservative moorings during the Bush years, particularly on earmarks and spending. It's been said that the Republicans were elected to change Washington, but instead, Washington changed them. A slew of scandals contributed to their loss of Congress in 2006, and the financial meltdown of 2008 paved the way for the national nightmare that is the Obama presidency.

Congressional Republicans, while never as overtly destructive as their Democratic counterparts, steadily lost their appetite for reform. After several productive years as the majority party, they began to act like Democrats. Voters grew tired of choosing the lesser of two evils, and they ultimately punished the Republicans. The GOP had to work hard to win back a skeptical nation.

To their everlasting credit, congressional Republicans took a united stand against government-run health care. For that, they're owed an enormous debt of gratitude and hopefully, the renewed confidence of the American people. The nation desperately needs a viable alternative to Obama—someone to vote *for*. After their performance at the health care summit, the Republican Party took a giant step toward credibility.

CHAPTER 18

AFTER THEIR MASSACHUSETTS FIASCO, nervous Democrats foresaw a gathering storm; a political tsunami threatening to swamp their congressional majority. Congress's approval rating plunged into the teens. Pelosi, who represents a San Francisco-based district that gave Obama over 85 percent of its vote, had a national approval rating of 11 percent. Senate Democratic leader Harry Reid of Nevada was in single digits.

Compounding the party's worries, Obama and Pelosi refused to give an inch on health care. Were this a game of poker, they'd be all-in. House Democrats were thus painted into a corner. They could vote for the Senate version, which meant agreeing to the special-interest provisions and assorted junk hastily crammed into the bill, not to mention federal funding of abortion. Or they could scrap the bill entirely, start over from scratch, and work with Republicans in a truly bipartisan manner.

Many rank-and-file Democrats came to an epiphany. If the bill were to pass, it would herald the end of the modern Democratic Party. Were it to fail, it would mark the end of the Obama presidency. As one freshman representative put it, it was like choosing your method of execution.

The final House vote was expected to be another nail-biter. The Chicago machine brought the full weight of the White House to bear on wavering representatives. Offers of pork programs, highway projects, presidential fundraising, and other perks rained down on undecided members. Meanwhile, the wrath of Obama and Pelosi awaited any Democrats who might dare to buck the administration.

Obama continued his manic drive for votes, offering increased water allotment to two undecided congressmen from agricultural districts in central California. The president even resorted to selling a federal judgeship: the brother of Representative Jim Matheson from Utah, who'd previously voted against ObamaCare, was appointed to the Tenth Circuit Court of Appeals. Representative Alan Mollohan of West Virginia had been under an FBI investigation for years for steering some $250 million to nonprofit organizations run by friends and real estate partners. Obama's Justice Department closed the inquiry in the middle of the health care debate.

We'll never know how many sleazy backroom deals were actually brokered in the all-out push for ObamaCare. Rumors circulated that cushy administration jobs were proffered to any representatives whose "yea" vote cost them re-election. (Such bribery isn't beneath the Chicago machine: Pennsylvania Democrat Joe Sestak claimed that administration officials offered him a high-level appointment if he'd withdraw his primary challenge to Specter. That's a felony.)

The arm-twisting became too much for some. Former Democratic Rep. Eric Massa of New York had this to say: "Rahm Emanuel is son of the devil's spawn. He is an individual who would sell his mother to get a vote. He would strap his children to the front end of a steam locomotive."

It was a massive push for a massive overhaul of a massive sector of the economy—and all to pass it on a narrow, party-line vote. "Hope and change" gave way to "divide and conquer."

STILL SHORT OF VOTES, congressional leaders attached certain "sweeteners" to the legislation, including a nationalization of student loans (in actuality, a hostile takeover of the student loan industry by the federal government). But the public pushed back hard. Congressional switchboards were jammed with so many calls in opposition to ObamaCare—as many as one hundred thousand per day—that many callers couldn't get through. One congressman admitted that calls to his office were running a hundred to one against the measure.

So desperate grew House leaders that, improbable though it may sound, they hatched a scheme to pass the Senate version without actually voting on it. You read that correctly: the Senate bill would simply be "deemed" to have passed the House. The ploy was unconstitutional on its face, yet Obama, the onetime constitutional law instructor, signed on to it. It came to be known as "deem and pass" (opponents took to calling it "demon-pass"). The House would vote on the more popular provisions of the Senate version, and then "deem" the entire bill to have passed.

Under pressure, Democrats abandoned the scheme. Even media allies became alarmed by their abuse of power. Remember, De Tocqueville predicted that loose fiscal policy will turn a democracy into a dictatorship. His words grow more prophetic by the day. *Is this really where Obama has taken us?* wondered an anxious nation.

When the dust finally settled, Obama got his way—again. On March 21, 2010, by a vote of 219-212, the House finally approved the Senate bill. ObamaCare officially became the law of the land.

The Stupak coalition caved under pressure, assuaged by an executive order prohibiting any federal funding of abortion. Their votes provided the margin of victory.

But the president's executive order isn't worth the paper it's written on, and his legal team knows it. As the Catholic bishops and the National Right to Life Committee pointed out, the courts have applied the principles of *Roe v. Wade* to federal health legislation unless Congress explicitly forbids such funding. In this instance, having eliminated the Stupak language, it did not do so.

"From a pro-life prospective, I find absolutely no comfort in this executive order. This puts the fate of the unborn in the hands of the most pro-abortion president in history," said Representative Joe Pitts, a Republican of Pennsylvania.

The outcome revealed that pro-life Democrats might talk a good game, but they cannot be trusted when the chips are down. Were Stupak and his allies duped by the executive order, or did they simply sell out? It was later reported that Obama promised Stupak more than $700,000 in grants for three airports in his district. (The Michigan congressman, his re-election prospects now fatally wounded, chose to retire rather than face the voters in the midterm elections.)

At least one member of the Stupak coalition, Democratic Representative Dan Lipinski of Illinois, held his ground. "I could not vote for a bill that would change the status quo on funding for abortion...But we weren't really voting for health reform. We were voting for a bill that is financially unsustainable," he said.

GOVERNMENT-RUN CARE WAS THUS a fait accompli. The nation's health care system, fully one-sixth of our economy, is now based on a rough draft of a bill written by the special interests. Not surprisingly, the final version was riddled with errors and oversights. One embarrassing miscue was the failure to include children in the provision relating to pre-existing conditions. This is what happens when politicians rush to pass a mammoth piece of legislation without understanding what's in it.

Even after passage, the new law continued to hemorrhage public support. A CBS poll taken a month later revealed that only about a third of Americans approved of the act. Voters in Missouri had a chance to weigh in on the law directly. In the state's August primary, a ballot measure that nullified the individual mandate to buy insurance, the heart of ObamaCare, passed with 71 percent of the vote. Missouri is an important bellwether state. Though the measure was largely symbolic, the outcome was an accurate gauge of national sentiment.

The bitter, year-long skirmish eroded Obama's standing and exposed his vulnerabilities. After some forty speeches, innumerable television appearances, and an enormous investment of political capital, his signature domestic priority passed with only a narrow majority. This president has managed to unite independents, libertarians, and fiscal and social conservatives against him. That's quite the hat trick. Can anyone remember a more poisonous political atmosphere? It didn't have to be this way, had he governed from the center. Yet Obama continues to lose the country, day by day. This is his legacy.

The corporate tax impact was felt immediately. AT&T and Verizon each anticipated a $1 billion-dollar charge due to the higher health care costs imposed by the law. Boeing expected to take a $150 million charge, Deere & Co. $150 million, Caterpillar Inc. $100 million, 3M $90 million, and so on.

Employees and customers alike will feel the sting. Expect layoffs and higher prices in the years to come. Student loan provider Sallie Mae said it would be forced to terminate more than 30 percent of its work force as a result of the student loan overhaul tucked into the legislation.

At least someone is hiring: Congress gave the IRS sweeping powers to enforce the new health care guidelines. Over sixteen thousand new agents will be needed to police ObamaCare alone. And at least someone is celebrating: Juan Lopez, chairman of the Communist Party USA, called the law a "historic victory" that will lead to socialized medicine.

CUE THE LITIGATION: elected officials in more than twenty states, along with the National Federation of Independent Business, have taken the remarkable step of filing lawsuits over the constitutionality of the law. Their main contention is the enormous financial burden being imposed on the states: an estimated fifteen million more Americans would be eligible for Medicaid under the law, potentially overwhelming state budgets. California, already grappling with a $20 billion deficit, will have to come up with billions more to cover additional enrollees.

Other legal questions abound. Where does the U.S. Constitution grant the federal government the power to force individuals to purchase health insurance? What other goods or services might the government require us to buy next? How much control can Uncle Sam exert over our everyday lives?

Seldom mentioned during the debate was the question over religious freedoms. The law actually carves out exemptions for two religious groups, Christian Scientists and the Amish. Can a federal law make specific exemptions for certain religious organizations, and not for others? What about conscience clauses for Baptist or Catholic workers? Or exemptions for Christians, Jews, and other people of faith who are morally opposed to abortion?

No enumerated power exists which grants Washington the authority to run health care. Nowhere in the Constitution is government empowered to make these deeply personal decisions. Rather, the Constitution was written to safeguard our rights *against* the government. If Obama has his way, the federal government would seize control of education, energy, broadcast media, and huge swaths of private industry, in violation of the Constitution.

We've drifted deep into uncharted territory. The federal government must now enforce a law which the majority of the governed neither wants nor supports. What happens if non-compliance becomes widespread? Or if states are literally unable to afford the mess that's been foisted upon them? The complexity of the law is as bewildering as the tax code. Will we need to hire accountants to explain its details?

Throughout history, virtually every successful legislative initiative has enjoyed broad, bipartisan support. Every Republican and thirty-four Democrats voted against final passage of ObamaCare. That doesn't augur well for its future. The fight over ObamaCare could make its way to the U.S. Supreme Court. Until then, or until the American people have a chance to repeal this monster, let's pray that our great republic avoids a constitutional crisis.

The outcome taught us an important lesson. The erosion of our liberties is the consequence of staying home on Election Day, throwing our vote away on a third-party long shot, or voting for *any* Democrat as some sort of a protest.

These are not your grandparents' Democrats. Make no mistake: today's party has been commandeered by the left-wing fringe.

CHAPTER 19

IT'S HARD TO DECIDE where Obama has done more damage: at home, centralizing the economy and consolidating his power, or abroad, apologizing on behalf of his country.

Obama's fascination with foreign audiences began in earnest during the presidential campaign. The young senator was running to be Commander in Chief of the United States Armed Forces, yet he lacked any foreign policy experience. To create the impression that Obama was at least semicompetent, his handlers sent him on an extended overseas junket in July 2008.

His trip to the Middle East and Europe was a media extravaganza unlike any in the annals of presidential politics. All three network anchors—Brian Williams, Charlie Gibson, and Katie Couric—along with a veritable who's who of American journalists, gleefully accompanied Obama on his adventure. The Democrat granted exclusive interviews to each anchor in different countries, affording them equal opportunities to serve as his public relations agent.

On a basketball court in Kuwait, to cheers from his media entourage, Obama sank a three-point shot. If there were ever an apt symbol for the whole Obama phenomenon—style, luck, and media adulation—this moment was it.

After photo ops with the troops in Iraq and Afghanistan, the candidate made his way to Germany, France, and Britain. The European leg of his tour was intended to repair relationships with our allies and burnish Obama's foreign policy credentials. His massive ego was on display before enormous crowds; Obama's speech at Berlin's Brandenburg Gate was attended by some two hundred thousand fans. The event had a "stop the presses" feeling back home. It was all Obama, all the time.

Meanwhile, an otherwise lackluster McCain campaign rolled out the best commercial of the year. The ad mocked Obama as "the biggest celebrity in the world" and asked, "But is he ready to lead?" It interspersed images of the Berlin speech with clips of Britney Spears and Paris Hilton, reinforcing the perception of the Democrat as a self-absorbed narcissist.

McCain had made three foreign trips in the preceding four months. None of the network hotshots tagged along. "The media has a bizarre fascination with Barack Obama," wrote the McCain camp in an e-mail. "The media is in love with Barack Obama. If it wasn't so serious, it would be funny."

One line from Obama's Berlin speech stands out: "Tonight, I speak to you…as a fellow citizen of the world."

The quote was remarkable in its significance. The expression "citizen of the world" was probably lost on most Americans, but Obama wasn't speaking to his countrymen; he was telegraphing a message to his international audience. It was a cryptic means of saying, "My nation is no more exceptional than any other." He was speaking in code, playing to the world's skepticism (or jealousy) of the United States.

It was a far, far cry from President Reagan's famous address at the same location, when the former president delivered the most memorable words of the Cold War: "Mr. Gorbachev, tear down this wall!"

Following the Brandenburg speech, now beloved by European leftists, Obama took on an aura of inevitability. With the election still four months away, he used a faux presidential seal and directed his aides to begin planning a White House transition. There wasn't enough sauerkraut in Germany to cover this hot dog.

OBAMA HOLDS A GRUDGE against his country, and he's not afraid to share it with the world. While attending a European summit in 2009, the newly-minted president was asked if he believed in American exceptionalism. "I believe in American exceptionalism, just as I suspect that the Brits believe in British exceptionalism, and the Greeks believe in Greek exceptionalism," was Obama's tepid response. That's as close to "no" as one can come without uttering the word.

Is it unreasonable to ask that a president convey a sense of pride in his country? Contrast Obama's answer with that of Florida's Marco Rubio, whose parents immigrated to the United States from Cuba: "I am privileged to be a citizen of the single greatest society in all of human history."

Even cynics were inspired by Reagan's optimism. George W. Bush, flaws and all, made no bones about his love of country. Had they been asked about American exceptionalism, Washington, Lincoln, Roosevelt, and Kennedy wouldn't have paused for a second. Then again, no one felt compelled to ask so obvious a question of an American president until Obama took office.

Obama has become one of the most polarizing figures in history. Call it a culture clash: his worldview counters that of the nation's conservative, patriotic majority. In Obama's mind, the United States is unjust, its wealth undeserved, its traditions discriminatory, its people uncultured, and its military imperialistic. He believes he was elected to re-engineer a fundamentally flawed society in his own left-wing, politically correct image. "You'll thank me later," is his brassy attitude.

To Obama, the United States is like an alcoholic beginning a twelve-step recovery program: the nation must first admit that it has a problem. He accomplished this by embarking upon an unprecedented worldwide apology tour. Obama was a disciplined campaigner; prior to the election, he'd managed to restrain himself. But after his inauguration, he was free to confess our nation's "sins" with abandon.

In his first three months of on-the-job training, Obama traveled to three continents to apologize to friend and foe alike. He granted the first formal interview of his presidency to a pan-Arab television network. "My job to the Muslim world is to communicate that the Americans are not your enemy. We sometimes make mistakes. We have not been perfect," declared the new president.

Obama also used the occasion to stress his own Muslim roots: "I have Muslim members of my family. I have lived in Muslim countries." This came as a surprise, since mention of Obama's Muslim ties during the election was regarded as fear-mongering.

The next stop on the apology tour was France. Mustering his most condescending tone, the new commander in chief took a cheap shot at his predecessor: "In America, there's a failure to appreciate Europe's leading role in the world. Instead of celebrating your dynamic union and seeking to partner with you to meet common challenges, there have been times where America has shown arrogance and been dismissive, even derisive."

Then it was back to the Middle East to explain his rejection of American exceptionalism to the Turkish Parliament: "The United States is still working through some of our own darker periods in our history…

Our country still struggles with the legacies of slavery and segregation, the past treatment of Native Americans."

Dredging up ancient history and reopening old wounds (on foreign soil, no less) served absolutely no diplomatic purpose. Leaders the world over were puzzled by Obama's gratuitous criticism of his own nation. It certainly didn't win over our enemies, especially in a powder keg like the Middle East. Foes interpreted it as a sign of weakness. Some, particularly in the Arab world, viewed such actions as a moral shortcoming on the part of a leader.

Obama also angered Christians when he made this statement in Turkey: "Whatever we once were, we are no longer a Christian nation [long pause] "at least, not 'just'…We are also a Jewish nation, a Muslim nation, a Buddhist nation, and a Hindu nation, and a nation of nonbelievers."

The line was fraught with innuendo. At best, it was political correctness gone mad; at worst, a forswearing of our founding principles. *Why does this man keep sticking his finger in our eye?* wondered his countrymen.

Back on U.S. soil, Obama apologized for the war on terror: "Unfortunately, faced with an uncertain threat, our government made a series of hasty decisions. I believe that many of these decisions were motivated by a sincere desire to protect the American people. But I also believe that all too often our government made decisions based on fear rather than foresight, that all too often our government trimmed facts and evidence to fit ideological predispositions."

He sought forgiveness for our treatment of terrorists: "Guantanamo set back the moral authority that is America's strongest currency in the world."

The apology tour wound its way to Latin America. "Too often, the United States has not pursued and sustained engagement with our neighbors. We have been too easily distracted by other priorities, and have failed to see that our own progress is tied directly to progress throughout the Americas," Obama opined in an editorial.

Speaking at the Summit of the Americas in Trinidad and Tobago, the president said, "While the United States has done much to promote peace and prosperity in the hemisphere, we have at times been disengaged, and at times we sought to dictate our terms."

At the summit, Obama greeted Marxist dictator Hugo Chávez in Spanish, exchanging handshakes and a friendly pat on the back. The Venezuelan despot, who has sought to destabilize democratically elected U.S. allies in Colombia and elsewhere, presented Obama a copy of *Open Veins of Latin America: Five Centuries of the Pillage of a Continent*. The publicity transformed the book, which virulently denounces U.S. policy in the hemisphere, into an international best-seller.

Also of note was a moment in which Obama, for once, wasn't talking. Another Marxist leader, Daniel Ortega of Nicaragua, addressed the summit for nearly an hour, delivering a blistering anti-U.S., anticapitalism tirade. Obama sat in silence throughout. Asked about the speech afterward, he offered no rebuttal, no defense of his country. When our president spoke the least, he may have said the most.

WHAT EVER BECAME OF the war on terror under this administration?

The incoming president believed the expression "Global War on Terror," enacted under Bush, was too insensitive (toward whom, the terrorists?). In an inexplicable nod to political correctness, Obama ordered that the phrase was to be renamed "Overseas Contingency Operations." Similarly, the word "terrorism" would be replaced by "man-caused disaster." All references to "Islamic radicalism" and "jihad" have been removed from Obama's national security documents. "Rogue" states are now labeled "outliers."

It sounds like a *Saturday Night Live* spoof, but the president was being serious. The new phraseology was adopted because, according to Homeland Security Secretary Janet Napolitano, the country needs to move away from the "politics of fear." Well, anyone who didn't feel fear—along with anger, sadness, and, yes, patriotism—after 9/11 ought to check his or her pulse. Then again, this administration behaves as though 9/11 never happened.

In Napolitano, the president selected a secretary of homeland security who had zero experience in national security, but who has shown herself to be worried about style and syntax (which is about as reassuring as her agency's pat-downs of third graders and elderly nuns at airport security). On behalf of the administration, Napolitano released a memo to law enforcement agencies warning that "right wingers" and "disgruntled veterans" represent possible threats to the country. It is disturbing to think Homeland Security might be keeping closer tabs on our returning veterans than on Islamic extremists.

THE OBAMA ADMINISTRATION KEPT its promise to the liberal netroots, swapping the tough Bush-Cheney antiterrorism policies for the same lax standards that made us so vulnerable. Under Clinton-era, pre-9/11 guidelines, FBI agents couldn't stake out mosques frequented by known terror suspects, and were barred from entering Internet chatrooms in which terrorism was being discussed. Agents grumbled that a crime had to be committed before they could act. The bureau was reactive instead of proactive.

Obama should thank his lucky stars that the Bush administration so effectively routed al-Qaeda worldwide. Bush regarded 9/11 as an act of war, not a criminal action, as Clinton treated the first World Trade

Center bombing in 1993, and embarked on an all-out campaign to annihilate al-Qaeda.

The irony is that Bush's success may have been his own undoing. By the end of his second term, with no further attacks on American soil in seven years, 9/11 became an increasingly distant memory for many voters. National security, arguably the greatest political asset for Bush and the Republican Party, was largely off the table by the fall of 2008. The nation's renewed sense of security thus set the stage for an untested, liberal newcomer to sweep into office.

That newcomer, Barack Obama, then undertook to purge the very national security policies which made his election possible. This has happened before. In 1992, after Reagan brought down the Soviet Union and ended the Cold War, foreign policy was no longer of paramount concern to the American people. The result was the election of a liberal Democrat, Bill Clinton, who proceeded to dismantle our intelligence capabilities while al-Qaeda established cells worldwide. It's interesting how history has a way of repeating itself.

CHAPTER 20

HILLARY CLINTON DREW BLOOD during the Democratic primaries with an ad called "3 AM," in which she questioned her rival's preparedness to respond to a national emergency at a moment's notice. Susan Rice, Obama's foreign policy adviser and current U.S. Ambassador to the United Nations, rose to her boss's defense on MSNBC—but she made a Freudian slip:

"Hillary Clinton hasn't had to answer the phone at three o'clock in the morning, and yet she attacked Barack Obama for not being ready. They're both not ready to have that 3 AM phone call."

AN INTEGRAL COMPONENT OF the war on terror is the Guantanamo Bay detention facility ("Gitmo"). The Bush administration used Gitmo to house the most hardened terrorists captured on the field of battle. A facility like Gitmo, though inherently imperfect, is essential to prosecuting a successful campaign against terrorism. Nowhere else could the United States properly house, interrogate, and try such dangerous enemy combatants.

However, Gitmo came to represent the far left's hatred of all things Bush, and Obama played to their passions. To wild ovations from his antiwar base, candidate Obama vowed to close Gitmo within a year of taking office. He lacked any plausible strategy for doing so—specifically, for housing Gitmo's inmates—but he plowed ahead with an executive order to close the facility.

Almost two years after his executive order, the president was still searching for a viable alternative to Gitmo. Obama has exhibited a pathological inability to acknowledge when he is wrong, even to the detriment to national security. Nowhere has that been more evident than in his quandary over Gitmo.

Obama hoped to convince foreign governments to accept charge of Gitmo's prisoners through the sheer power of his charisma. They declined. He then planned to move the detainees to federal prisons on U.S. soil, but was rebuffed by members of his own party. To date, the facility remains open and in an awkward state of limbo while Obama busies himself with other priorities. The dilemma over Guantanamo Bay is a symbol for the dangers of elevating a rookie to an office for which he is wholly unprepared.

THE LEFT SAVAGED BUSH over wiretaps of terror suspects, but they forget that Lincoln and Roosevelt also intercepted enemy transmissions during times of war. The Bush administration's policies of warrantless wiretaps and enhanced interrogation of terrorists were responsible for preventing further attacks after 9/11, including a plot to blow up the Brooklyn Bridge at rush hour. This doesn't seem to matter to President Obama, a vociferous critic of the practices. To him, protecting the civil liberties of terrorists takes priority over national security considerations.

Enhanced interrogation techniques, derided as "torture" by critics, enabled the intelligence community to foil plots to destroy the U.S. Consulate in Karachi and the Marine camp in Djibouti, and to fly hijacked airplanes into buildings in London and Los Angeles. They resulted in the detentions of thousands of dangerous enemy combatants and provided invaluable intelligence to our soldiers on the battlefield.

Critics argue that techniques such as waterboarding violate the Geneva Convention. But they have it oh-so-wrong. Al-Qaeda terrorists were not forcibly conscripted into a recognized national military; they *chose* to fight out of a perverse religious conviction. As such, they are not, nor have ever been, subject to the terms of the Geneva Convention.

Obama believes otherwise; he would extend the court of law to the field of battle. Henceforth, when interrogating enemy combatants, CIA agents are required to abide by the Army Field Manual, thereby assuring that terrorists receive better treatment than criminals at a police station.

Enhanced interrogation is not the same as torture. The techniques leave no physical scars, do no long-term damage, and never put anyone's life at risk. During waterboarding, for instance, a medical doctor is always standing by. If a detainee cooperated, he was never subjected to enhanced techniques in the first place; it was purely his choice. Critics tend to overlook this.

Besides, the overwhelming majority of interrogation techniques were far more moderate than waterboarding. Requiring prisoners to stand for long periods, adjusting the temperature in their cells, and playing rap music were common practices. (Well, maybe the rap music really was torture.)

Only three al-Qaeda figures were waterboarded by the CIA, one of whom was 9/11 mastermind Khalid Sheikh Mohammed (KSM), who refused to respond to milder techniques. The waterboarding finally broke him: "I was responsible for the 9/11 operation, from A to Z," he told interrogators. KSM also admitted to helping organize the 1993 World Trade Center attack, the Bali nightclub bombings, the beheading of reporter Daniel Pearl, and the attempted "shoe bombing" by Richard Reid, as well as planning attacks against Heathrow Airport and Big Ben in London. Come to think of it, waterboarding may have been too kind for this monster.

Obama wasn't content to eviscerate Bush's successful intelligence and antiterrorism policies. His administration drew up plans to prosecute agents who conducted the interrogations and the attorneys who advised them. The men whose efforts saved so many American lives now found themselves in the government's crosshairs. This shows the vindictive side of Obama.

Fortunately, no action has been taken as yet—Obama may have been talked down from the ledge—but that excuses nothing. The president and his attorney general left these brave men dangling for months under the threat of prosecution. That's unforgivable.

Doing so would have established a dangerous precedent under which officials of one administration could be harassed by the next, even if they were proffering legal advice based on their reading of the law (in this case, the USA PATRIOT Act, which was duly passed by Congress in 2001). This is to be expected in third-world dictatorships— one can imagine the likes of Chávez persecuting political opponents in a like manner—but not the United States.

What explains Obama's irrational quest for the blood of our own agents? It has been suggested that, owing to his paternal lineage, Obama's sympathies for the Muslim world prejudice his policies. Either way, something deeper and darker is clearly lurking for the man to stoop to such a level.

OBAMA'S OBSESSION WITH EXTENDING constitutional protections to terrorists culminated in his administration's decision to try KSM and four other defendants in civilian court, as opposed to military tribunals, as planned by Bush. The trials would be held in New York City, just blocks from Ground Zero.

Even liberal New Yorkers were outraged over the Justice Department's treatment of the al-Qaeda heavyweight. In civilian court, KSM and the other terrorists would be provided legal counsel, courtesy of the taxpayers, along with all the rights bestowed on any criminal defendant. The trials would be open to the public, which could force the release of CIA records and confidential memos. That could compromise the identity of undercover agents and gravely jeopardize the war on terror—oops, overseas contingency operations.

KSM won't be the only terrorist to appear in civilian court. Obama's Justice Department likewise chose to try Umar Farouk Abdulmutallab, the so-called "Christmas Day" or "underwear" bomber, in civilian court. Seems a military tribunal might be too harsh for him, too.

After attempting to detonate his device aboard a crowded aircraft, the underwear bomber was read his Miranda rights, including the right to an attorney and the right to remain silent. After initially volunteering information, Abdulmutallab lawyered up and quieted down. Whereas Bush would have shipped Abdulmutallab off to Gitmo for some private time with the CIA's finest, Obama elected to treat him as a criminal defendant.

The near-success of the underwear bomber also revealed glaring weaknesses in the administration's more "sensitive" antiterrorism procedures. Abdulmutallab's father notified the State Department that his son had become radicalized, was spouting anti-American rhetoric, and had trained with terrorists in Yemen. However, that wasn't enough to get him onto even a low-level terrorist watch list. (Great Britain, acting on lesser intelligence, banned Abdulmutallab from entering the country.)

"The Obama administration appears to have a blind spot when it comes to the war on terror. This administration cannot see a foreign terrorist even when he stands right in front of them, fresh from an attempt to blow a plane out of the sky on Christmas Day." That statement didn't come from some right-wing hawk, but from Senator Susan Collins, sometime ally of the president.

Obama is loathe to use the words "Muslim" and "terrorist" in the same sentence. You won't hear this president talk about Islamic extremism; it's not in his vocabulary. In fact, he didn't address the nation for three days after the attempted Christmas Day bombing. He let Napolitano do his talking: "The system worked," she famously declared, doing her best Keystone Kops impression.

Abdulmutallab was the third terrorist to plan an attack on U.S. soil on Obama's watch. The first, Muslim convert Abdulhakim Muhammad, opened fire on a military recruiting office in Little Rock, Arkansas, killing one person and wounding another in June 2009.

The second, Major Nidal Malik Hasan, carried out an even deadlier attack five months later. Hasan gunned down thirteen innocents and wounded thirty-two others at Fort Hood Army Base in Texas.

With the press assembled, Obama gave a statement on the Fort Hood tragedy. First however, he praised a cabinet official and other bureaucrats in attendance, and then gave a "shout out" to a Congressional Medal of Honor recipient. After rambling for two minutes, the president finally got around to mentioning the shootings.

The wounded troops did get a secret presidential visit—from former President Bush, with no press coverage. Imagine Obama traveling anywhere without a full media entourage.

Obama's seeming indifference to the massacre raised eyebrows. Could he be this aloof and detached? Was it a reflection, however subconscious, of his attitude toward the military? Or is the man simply uncomfortable discussing an act of Islamic terrorism?

The administration set out to whitewash any mention of the shooter's religion. Its after-action report failed to note that Hasan is a Muslim, that his business card identified him as a "Soldier of Allah," or that he shouted "Allahu Akbar" (*God is great,* the cry of an Islamic martyr) while murdering his victims.

Joe Lieberman, chairman of the Senate Homeland Security Committee, requested additional information related to the Fort Hood massacre, but administration officials remained mysteriously unforthcoming. Having been stonewalled, Lieberman and Collins, the committee's ranking member, discussed taking their subpoena fight to court.

"If they won't respond, I think we have an obligation. It's not easy to enforce a subpoena against the executive branch, but I'm going to make the fight," said Lieberman.

"The administration just does not want to cooperate, and I think that's just really unfortunate," added Collins.

Those promises of transparency and open government sounded great during the campaign. It's a shame Obama didn't mean a word of it.

A FOURTH ATTEMPT AT TERRORISM occurred in May, 2010 when Faisal Shahzad, a Muslim Pakistani American, parked an SUV filled with explosives in New York City's Times Square. Fortunately, they failed to detonate. Had it not been for Shahzad's incompetence— and a couple of sharp-eyed street vendors—hundreds of people could have lost their lives. Shahzad was apprehended while trying to flee the country.

Liberals first sought to blame Tea Party activists upset with the government takeover of health care, for the attempted bombing. When that was disproved, they rushed to downplay the suspect's ties to Islam. When it was revealed that Shahzad was trained by the Pakistani Taliban, the administration decided to claim credit for thwarting the attack.

"We're not lucky, we're good," crowed White House counterterrorism adviser John Brennan.

Countered Lieberman: "We *were* lucky. We did not prevent the attempted attack."

The Times Square car bombing attempt—the fourth would-be terrorist act in Obama's young presidency—left many questioning whether this administration even has a comprehensive antiterrorism plan. Is the president motivated more by ideology than reality? Does he convey weakness? Did his election embolden Islamic extremists?

Is this administration sufficiently competent to protect the American people? Under the circumstances, these are all legitimate questions. The early returns are not encouraging.

CHAPTER 21

IN 2007, OBAMA WAS ONE of just fourteen senators to vote against funding the troops in Afghanistan and Iraq. He complained that the Bush administration hadn't laid out a withdrawal date, and he protested by voting against the men and women in uniform.

Then-rival Biden accused Obama of playing politics with national security: "And I want to ask any of my other colleagues, would they, in fact, vote to cut off the money for those troops to protect them? That's the right question. This isn't cutting off the war. This is cutting off support that will save the lives of thousands of American troops."

Republicans called the vote the equivalent of waving a white flag to al-Qaeda. Perhaps it was a harbinger of things to come.

Four years into the Iraq War, sectarian violence continued to endanger the military and political gains made by coalition forces. To counter this threat, the bipartisan Iraq Study Group counseled a surge. "The United States should significantly increase the number of U.S. military personnel, including combat troops, imbedded in and supporting Iraqi Army units," the panel reported.

President Bush followed its recommendation, sending thirty thousand additional troops to Baghdad and Al Anbar in early 2007. McCain and Lieberman, among others, had been pushing for an aggressive counterinsurgency strategy for years.

In response to the president's action, the Senate, newly controlled by Democrats, took up a nonbinding resolution in opposition to the troop surge. Obama voted in lockstep with the chamber's liberals; he predicted the surge would lead to a further escalation of violence and would fail to stabilize the situation on the ground. Once more, Obama's position conceded defeat. McCain characterized the vote as an insult to every soldier who'd fought in Iraq.

The surge was essential for Iraq's continued development into a stable, oil-rich democracy in the heart of the Middle East. And it was an unbridled success: by the end of 2009, civilian deaths fell to their lowest level since the war began. In December of that year, no U.S. combat deaths were recorded. Sectarian violence fell dramatically throughout the country.

Even the *New York Times*, a leading critic of the war, grudgingly acknowledged as much: "The surge, clearly, has worked…The result, now visible in the streets, is a calm unlike any the country has seen since the American invasion…The signs—Iraqi families flooding into parks at sundown, merchants throwing open long-shuttered shops—are stunning to anyone who witnessed the country's implosion in 2005 and 2006."

McCain pounced: "Today, we know Senator Obama was wrong. The surge has succeeded. And because of its success, the next president will inherit a situation in Iraq in which America's enemies are on the run, and our soldiers are beginning to come home."

Obama would never admit that he'd erred, of course. Even while running for president, he maintained his mulish opposition to the surge.

Were this any other candidate, particularly one so thoroughly inexperienced, such an epic foreign policy misjudgment would have doomed his presidential aspirations. Yet Obama, who has more lives than a cat, emerged unscathed.

After the election, Obama admitted to General David Petraeus, chief architect of the surge, that his strategy had worked brilliantly. Not only that, but the Obama White House started taking credit for the success in Iraq! Biden boasted of the drawdown in U.S. forces: "You're going to see ninety thousand American troops come marching home by the end of the summer." He was referring to a withdrawal schedule which had been negotiated between Bush and Prime Minister Maliki in late 2008.

"I am very optimistic about Iraq," continued Biden. "You're going to see a stable government in Iraq that is actually moving toward a representative government. I mean, this could be one of the great achievements of this administration."

This administration! That's one heaping helping of chutzpah.

ON THE EIGHTH ANNIVERSARY of the Afghanistan war, General Stanley McChrystal also requested a troop surge to help defeat al-Qaeda and the stubbornly resilient Taliban. After three interminable months of indecision, Obama finally agreed to send an additional thirty thousand troops to Afghanistan in late 2009.

The drawback was that Obama simultaneously announced an eighteen-month timetable for withdrawing the reinforcements. Whereas Bush never allowed himself to be boxed in by arbitrary deadlines, Obama signaled that his commitment is temporary and conditional. Al-Qaeda has waited us out before, and they can wait us out again. The enemy is well aware that many Americans, and particularly our media, have little patience for long-term military engagements.

Obama's pussyfooting clearly piqued McChrystal, the top U.S. commander in Afghanistan. In an article in *Rolling Stone* magazine in June 2010, McChrystal aired his frustrations with Obama's dysfunctional civilian team. The general ridiculed the "wimps in the White House" and described the president as uncomfortable, intimidated, and unengaged during their initial meeting.

Military experts were amazed that a distinguished thirty-seven-year veteran would volunteer such a scathing assessment of his bosses. It was a remarkable event, virtually without precedent. Didn't McChrystal realize he was unleashing a firestorm? Or was that his intention? Does his critique reflect a larger sentiment among military brass? Also left unanswered were questions over Obama's muddled Afghanistan policy: is he serious about winning this war?

McChrystal issued a terse apology, but was relieved of his duties shortly thereafter. It marked the first time that a president has ousted a wartime commander since Truman fired MacArthur in 1951.

OBAMA'S FIRST INTERNATIONAL CRISIS came three months into his presidency when Somali pirates took American cargo ship Captain Richard Phillips hostage off the Horn of Africa. The president gave the order for navy SEAL snipers to take out the pirates and rescue the captain. Americans were relieved by the outcome. The media were especially overflowing with praise over Obama's handling of the situation.

Lost in the hoopla that week, fortuitously for Obama, was a more ominous threat: North Korea test-fired a missile designed to carry nuclear warheads into the Pacific. Obama's response to the act was to announce deep cuts in the U.S. missile defense program. It was like something out of a bad spy novel.

The launch was no accident. North Korea and other rogue regimes have tracked this president's actions, since his inauguration, with an eagle eye. Obama's foreign policy is largely rhetorical—he's been called the National Public Radio president—thus emboldening the likes of North Korea's Kim Jong-il to pursue his nuclear weapons program. Officially, the communist leader was testing a missile. Unofficially, he was testing the new American president.

As with its prosecution of the war in Afghanistan and the fight against Islamic terrorism, the Obama administration appears to have no comprehensive plan for dealing with emerging nuclear threats like North Korea and Iran—and their leaders know it. Dictators can smell weakness an ocean away.

At a Democratic presidential debate sponsored by CNN and YouTube, Obama was asked the following: "Would you be willing to meet separately, without precondition, during the first year of your administration, with the leaders of Iran, Syria, Venezuela, Cuba, and North Korea?"

His answer was unequivocal: "I would. And the reason is this: the notion that somehow not talking to countries is punishment to them, which has been the guiding diplomatic principle of [the Bush] adminis-tration, is ridiculous."

It was an amateur response. Perhaps unbeknown to Obama, the United States talks to its adversaries on a regular basis; midlevel inter-mediaries have been negotiating to dismantle Iran's nuclear capabilities for years. The question was whether the commander in chief himself should enhance the stature of a foreign dictator by granting him a one-on-one meeting.

Obama's oft-repeated pledge implied a willingness to meet with Iranian President Mahmoud Ahmadinejad, a Holocaust denier who is committed to wiping Israel off the map. Ahmadinejad's Iran is a state sponsor of terror in Iraq and Afghanistan, and he's working to develop nuclear weaponry in defiance of U.N. Security Council resolutions.

Granting an audience to such a madman is beneath the dignity of the president of the United States. Such a mind-set telegraphs naiveté, and Hillary Clinton pummeled Obama over it. "We simply cannot legitimize rogue regimes or weaken American prestige by impulsively agreeing to presidential talks that have no preconditions," said Obama's fellow Democrat.

Clinton also criticized Obama for opposing a Senate resolution which designated Iran's Revolutionary Guard a "terrorist organization." (It would seem like a no-brainer, but in the Democratic primaries, where peaceniks dominate, Obama's sophomoric stance on the resolution earned him political currency.)

The grownups recommended ramping up sanctions against Iran, while keeping the military option on the table. Obama chose instead to extend a hand, convinced that his nice-guy routine would be a game-changer in the Middle East. Ahmadinejad responded by mocking Obama as a novice and a paper tiger. "Wait until your sweat dries and you get some experience," taunted the Iranian president, who is dangerously close to realizing his nuclear ambitions.

AT SUCH A HAZARDOUS PERIOD in American history, Obama's first State of the Union address gave remarkably short shrift to international affairs. What little he did say was wanting.

The president spoke vaguely about "growing consequences" to Iran for its uranium enrichment program, but never outlined a course of action. He failed to credit the protesters who were murdered by Ahmadinejad's forces in Iran's sham elections, and he ignored calls for human rights protections in that country and elsewhere. Terrorism went virtually unmentioned in the address, but he did find time to call for relaxing the ban on gays serving in the military. What does this reveal about his priorities?

Even as a senator, Obama's attention was focused everywhere but on foreign policy. After assuming the chairmanship of the Foreign Relations Subcommittee on European Affairs, which has jurisdiction over NATO's role in Afghanistan and Iraq, he never convened a policy hearing. The subcommittee serves as a research-gathering body for the Senate as a whole, but Obama failed to hold so much as a single hearing. Nor did he travel to Europe on any fact-finding missions during his chairmanship, that is, until his mammoth media spectacle during his presidential campaign. Prior to that, he'd visited Iraq only once. (McCain made eight trips to Iraq since the start of the war.)

The word *victory* rarely crosses Obama's lips during his foreign policy pronouncements. He devoted about a paragraph in his State of the Union address to the Afghan troop surge, never bringing himself to mention victory. Allies and enemies alike knew that Bush possessed a single-mindedness of purpose, which was to achieve victory. His successor isn't instilled with that same drive and determination.

CHAPTER 22

A S THE WORLD'S DOMINANT nuclear superpower, the United States hasn't used such weaponry since World War II. Our nuclear arsenal has served as an effective deterrent against foreign aggression. It was President Reagan who championed the doctrine of "peace through strength."

Obama, like most liberal Democrats, doesn't get this. He has called for the elimination of nuclear arms worldwide, and he seeks to narrow the circumstances under which the United States might utilize nuclear weaponry.

"Speak softly and carry a big stick" was President Theodore Roosevelt's famous mantra. Obama's might be: "Speak often and unilaterally disarm." A powerful nuclear arsenal is the biggest stick of all; it is mankind's greatest deterrent to war.

Breaking with his predecessors, Obama announced a new nuclear posture: if attacked, the United States will not use nuclear weapons against states which abide by the Nuclear Non-Proliferation Treaty (NNPT). This policy holds even if we're hit with chemical or biological weapons, both of which are cheaper and easier for rogue regimes to acquire than nukes. Nearly every nation in the world has signed the NNPT, the notable exceptions being Iran and North Korea. Even a Taliban-controlled Afghanistan wouldn't qualify for nuclear retaliation under Obama's new guidelines.

Jimmy Carter, inept leader that he was, never went this far. The expressed policy of previous administrations of both parties was to use nuclear arms "to deter a wide range of threats." Obama single-handedly rewrote the rules of engagement, tipping his hand to our enemies in the process. Even French President Nicolas Sarkozy has been openly critical of his stance. "We live in a real world, not a virtual world," a frustrated Sarkozy told Obama at a U.N. Security Council meeting. (Something's amiss when France takes a harder line than the United States.)

Obama also forswore development of new weapons, a position even his secretary of defense opposed. Nuclear weapons deteriorate over time and need to be replaced. Thanks to our nuclear superiority, the United States has weaned itself away from chemical and biological weaponry. If Obama has his way, that critical advantage will be lost.

To our enemies, Obama is the gift that keeps on giving. His vision of a nuclear-free world obviously isn't shared by rogue states seeking nuclear weaponry—Iran and North Korea—or by world powers already stocked with them—Russia, China, and India.

"I will slow our development of future combat systems...and achieve deep cuts in our nuclear arsenals," stated Obama in an online message to supporters. What does he propose to do if the United States is attacked—make another speech?

This president is fond of saying that words matter. He's right: his words convey a sense of weakness to the world at large. International adulation is not to be mistaken for respect.

AS IF ROGUE REGIMES and Islamic extremism aren't enough to worry about, traditional rivals like Russia and China are scouring this president's actions and words for any perceived weakness. They needn't strain their eyes.

Obama wasted little time in his quest for unilateral disarmament. In April 2010, he signed a major strategic arms reduction treaty with Russia. The treaty, known as New START, would reduce both nations' stockpiles of nuclear weapons.

The United States was the stronger of the two powers, yet we negotiated from a position of weakness. In contrast to his Russian counterparts—President Dmitry Medvedev and Prime Minister Vladimir Putin, the ex-KGB operative—Obama brings a 1960s-era, antinuclear bias to arms negotiations. The political neophyte was clearly out of his league when negotiating with the crafty, battle-scarred Russian bosses. (Why cede anything to a novice who's obviously hankering for a treaty?) In keeping with Obama administration policy, negotiations were conducted in secret. Congress hadn't even seen the treaty prior to the signing ceremony.

The United States can expect to make the lion's share of reductions. To remedy the imbalance between the nations, the treaty obliges the United States to dismantle some 150 delivery platforms, while Russia is permitted to *add* 130 such vehicles. We are also required to scrap eighty more warheads than our timeworn rival. Worse, the Russians have a long history of reneging on arms agreements, especially when credible verification is next to impossible. The treaty will buy time for Russia and China to upgrade their aging arsenals while we're disassembling ours.

If that's not cause for heartburn, Obama says New START only "sets the stage" for further arms reductions. He's already initiated negotiations with the Russians on limiting shorter-range missiles.

This president is intent on eviscerating our nuclear superiority and with it, quite possibly, our superpower status. Carter's appeasement of the old Soviet Union contributed to the destabilization of Europe, Asia, Africa, and Latin America. Those who have not learned from history are doomed to repeat it. Was Obama sleeping through the Cold War?

OBAMA ALSO DEALT A BLOW to our eastern European allies by canceling an antiballistic missile (ABM) system designed to protect Poland and the Czech Republic. President Bush proposed the shield to defend the region from rogue states; it is estimated that Iran will have developed an intercontinental ballistic missile (ICBM) capable of reaching Europe by 2015. Our allies have no defense against such a scenario.

Russia opposed the ABM system, perceiving it as a threat against its dominance of the region. Obama kowtowed to their objections, hoping to score points with Moscow in the tug-of-war over Iran's nuclear enrichment program. For revealing the United States to be a fickle partner, Obama gained nothing. From an economic standpoint, Medvedev and Putin have no incentive to antagonize the Iranian regime. It was another diplomatic mess attributable to the president's callowness.

Poland, the Czech Republic, and other former Soviet-bloc nations have been among our most stalwart allies, eternally grateful to the United States for liberating them from the scourge of communism. They've returned the favor by standing shoulder to shoulder with us in the war on terror. Yet Obama sold out our eastern European partners to a higher bidder. They must be thinking, *with friends like this*...

IS OBAMA ANTI-ISRAEL? Since his emergence as a credible presidential contender, Obama's friendships with Khalidi, the rabidly anti-Semitic professor, and Rev. Wright, who openly embraced Nation of Islam leader Louis Farrakhan, have worried supporters of the

Jewish state. Then there is the matter of Obama's own paternal lineage: his father and stepfather were both Muslims. The president's defenders argue that such imputation is unfair.

Candidate Obama actively courted the Jewish vote by portraying himself as a staunch supporter of Israel. But since taking office, Obama's policies toward America's only democratic ally in the Middle East have painted a darker picture.

According to Israel's ambassador to the United States, relations with Washington have reached a historic low under Obama. Surveys reveal that only 4 percent of Israelis believe Obama's policies are more pro-Israel than either pro-Palestinian or neutral. While 78 percent of Jewish Americans voted for Obama in 2008, a poll by the McLaughlin Group two years later showed that barely half that number would vote to re-elect him.

Despite Israel's consent to a two-state deal with the Palestinians, Obama treats the small nation as the obstacle to peace. The pressure is always on the Israelis to offer more concessions; the more they offer, the more the Palestinians demand, with White House approval. Based on their reading of the Koran, members of Hamas (a terrorist organization which holds a majority of seats in the Palestinian Parliament) object to the very existence of Israel. Backed by a soon-to-be nuclear Iran, they are unappeasable. We've forced our ally into a no-win situation.

Israel's need to provide housing for its growing population prompted a diplomatic skirmish with the Obama administration. When Israel's enemies demanded that it cease all new construction in East Jerusalem, the United States accused Israel of sabotaging the peace process. Never mind that Jerusalem is the holiest city in Judaism, the land is entirely within Israel's borders, and that Jews have lived there for three thousand years; Obama has shown no reluctance to micromanage Israel's affairs.

The consequence was a puerile snub of Prime Minister Benjamin Netanyahu during a White House visit in early 2010. Netanyahu was left to wait for over an hour while the president finished dinner. When Obama finally emerged, he tersely presented the Israeli leader with a list of thirteen demands, one of which was to halt all new construction. Obama refused to allow the meeting to be photographed, no joint appearances were made, and no formal statement was issued.

The chilly reception was intended to weaken Netanyahu's standing at home, thus forcing him to accept even greater Palestinians demands. Obama's behavior toward Israel's democratically elected leader contrasts with the respect and patience shown Islamic extremists in the region (one can't imagine him treating Ahmadinejad with such pettiness). This president has a maddening penchant for treating our enemies with deference, and our allies with contempt.

OBAMA'S RESENTMENT TOWARD Great Britain, our oldest, closest, and arguably most important friend, is the product of his family history. His paternal grandfather, Hussein Onyango Obama, was imprisoned and allegedly tortured by the British during the struggle for Kenyan independence in 1949. Sarah Onyango ("Granny Sarah" to young Barack) said this about her husband's imprisonment: "We realized that the British were actually not friends but, instead, enemies."

Hussein Onyango's lifelong hatred of the British was handed down to his son, Barack Sr., who viewed them as despised colonialists. He too was arrested by the British for involvement in the independence movement, but was released within a matter of days. Barack Sr. took part in a U.S.-sponsored program to train Kenyans to run their own country after independence (ironically, that's how he ended up at the University of Hawaii). Two generations of hatred were not lost on Barack Jr.

President Obama committed a series of diplomatic faux pas—dubbed "gift gaffe" in the United Kingdom—with British leaders. It is an age-old tradition that newly-elected leaders exchange gifts that are symbolic of the relationship between the nations. Prime Minister Gordon Brown gave Obama a pen holder made from the timbers of the Victorian antislavery ship HMS *Gannet*, a framed commission for the HMS *Resolute*, and a first edition of the seven-volume biography of Churchill.

In turn, Obama gave Brown a set of twenty-five American DVDs which don't work on European machines.

The president outdid himself by presenting Queen Elizabeth with a video iPod—loaded with his speeches, no less—which could have been purchased at Walmart. (The Queen had one already.) The president further raised eyebrows when he returned a famous bust of Winston Churchill loaned to the White House after 9/11. Gift gaffe went largely unnoticed stateside, but it was a big deal in Britain. At best, it was tacky; at worst, it embodied the low esteem in which the commander in chief holds our closest ally.

On the diplomatic front, Obama snubbed Brown on his first visit by canceling the traditional Rose Garden ceremony between the leaders. White House officials claimed the president was "overwhelmed" by the economic meltdown and unable to focus on foreign policy. The slight left the British press seething.

Obama maintained a position of neutrality in Britain's conflict with Argentina over the Falklands, despite Britain's having fought by our side in Iraq and Afghanistan. Whereas Bush expressed his appreciation to British troops at every opportunity, Obama has never acknowledged our ally's contribution to the war on terror.

Clearly, the special relationship with the United Kingdom isn't so special to this president. Once more, Obama's personal hang-ups appear to hamper the United States' most important alliances.

On the subject of awkward snubs, Obama refused to meet with the Dalai Lama for months, even when the Tibetan spiritual leader traveled to Washington to meet with members of Congress. The communist Chinese were pressuring world leaders not to meet with him, and Obama acquiesced for over a year. Human rights groups viewed Obama's actions as appeasement: the president needs the Chinese to continue purchasing his debt.

Finally, Obama agreed to a meeting. As with Netanyahu, the session was kept hush-hush and no photographs were permitted. Afterward, the Dalai Lama was made to exit the White House through a rear service entrance. Obama hoped the Chinese wouldn't find out about the meeting, but photographs of the elderly monk traipsing past bags of trash made their way to the Drudge Report.

UNDER OBAMA'S LEADERSHIP, the United States has earned a reputation as an unpredictable and unreliable ally. One prominent Asian leader summarized the international concern accordingly: "We in Asia are convinced that Obama is not strong enough to confront his opponents, but we fear that he is not strong enough to support his friends."

An apt symbol of Obama's foreign policy is his bowing at the waist to foreign monarchs. His first bow was to King Abdullah of Saudi Arabia. Soon thereafter, he bowed to Japanese Emperor Akihito. Neither man reciprocated the gesture.

Eyes rolled and jaws dropped at the photographs of an American president bowing to a Muslim ruler. Democrats had a hard time explaining it, and even world leaders were puzzled by his actions. Obama might have missed the memo, but bowing to a foreign leader is universally regarded as an act of submission.

The American media glossed over the stories, and Obama was never called to account. Some pundits asked dismissively, "Does it really matter?"

Well, *of course* it matters.

Maybe if this president showed a little pride in his country, it wouldn't matter. As much.

CHAPTER 23

THIS PRESIDENT WAS SUPPOSED to be competent. His response to the oil leak in the Gulf of Mexico put that theory to rest.

The massive leak came to be known as Obama's Katrina, evoking unflattering comparisons to the Bush administration's sluggish response to the devastating 2005 hurricane. Given that Obama himself was one of Bush's harshest critics in the aftermath of Katrina, he is owed no greater deference. His detached, perfunctory response to his own Gulf crisis brought withering criticism from both ends of the political spectrum.

The BP (also known as British Petroleum) leak now ranks as the worst environmental catastrophe in the nation's history, surpassing even Three Mile Island in terms of projected long-range damage. Lost in the debate is the environmentalists' own culpability in the disaster: by opposing shallow-water and land-based drilling (including barren reaches of Alaska), they forced the oil rigs into deeper, more hazardous seas, where plugging the leak proved far more problematic.

As BP struggled ineptly to stem the flow of oil into the Gulf, Obama found time to attend Democratic fundraisers, host Paul McCartney at the White House, deliver commencement addresses, bash Republicans over financial regulatory reform, vacation in Maine, dine with the editor of *Vogue* magazine, appear on *The View*, and work on cutting a few strokes off his golf game.

The White House was briefed on the crisis within twenty-four hours of the explosion. Two weeks later, Obama finally got around to visiting the Gulf. To the frustration of local officials, his appearance turned into little more than a photo op. For two months, Obama didn't speak with the CEO of BP. To many, the leadership void was a painful reminder of the president's dearth of executive experience—and his failure to learn from the mistakes of his predecessor.

His erstwhile ally, Matthews, remarked that the president was "acting a little like a Vatican observer."

James Carville, a native Louisianan, wasn't as restrained: "I'm as good a Democrat as most…[But] they are risking everything by this 'go along with BP' strategy they have that seems like, lackadaisical on this, and…they seem like they're inconvenienced by this, this is some giant thing getting in their way and somehow or another, if you let BP handle it, it'll all go away."

That BP, a foreign entity, will go down as one of the great scoundrels in history is beyond question. But these are federal lands and federal leases; the president of the United States bears ultimate responsibility for the handling of the disaster. Obama's idea of leadership was to make the relief efforts all about him: "My job right now is just to make sure that everybody in the Gulf understands this is what I wake up to in the morning, and this is what I go to bed at night thinking about: the spill."

The president also regaled his audience with the odd—and, no doubt, fabricated—story of his daughter asking, "Have you plugged the hole yet, Daddy?"

A flustered Obama took to language befitting a Chicago street hustler: "We talk to these folks…so I know whose ass to kick." To the narcissistic mind, such rhetorical bluster constitutes leadership. It was not, however, what the coastal states desperately needed.

"At least a dozen federal agencies have taken part in the spill response, making decision-making slow, conflicted, and confused..." wrote the *New York Times*.

The *Washington Post* reported that the administration "saw no need to accept offers of state-of-the-art skimmers, miles of boom, or technical assistance from nations around the globe with experience fighting oil spills."

The consul general for the Netherlands in Houston had this to say: "The embassy got a nice letter from the administration that said, 'Thanks, but no thanks.'"

Florida officials begged for additional skimmers, but the century-old, protectionist Jones Act prevented foreign vessels from aiding in cleanup efforts. Three months into the crisis, Obama still hadn't waived the Act (Bush did so during Katrina) and those foreign ships sat idle. The president's logic wasn't entirely clear, but many believe it was a sop to maritime labor unions, who view foreign involvement as competition.

"We are still receiving reports of foreign-flagged vessels being turned away or their offers of assistance hanging in limbo. That should not be the case. There is a breakdown of communication," wrote Senator George LeMieux of Florida.

Louisiana Governor Bobby Jindal sought permission to construct a network of sand berms to protect the state's beaches and fragile marshlands. Federal officials dragged their feet, finally granting permission to only part of Jindal's request. (And why, exactly, do we want these same bureaucrats running health care?)

This was an emergency situation, and Obama could have cut through the red tape and demanded immediate action. Instead, he chose not to let the crisis go to waste.

After weeks of passing the blame, the president issued a six-month moratorium on deep-water drilling, a rash decision which killed thousands of jobs and further crippled the battered Gulf Coast economy. He also canceled or suspended drilling off the coasts of Alaska and Virginia, and suggested raising taxes on all oil companies as a punishment. Naturally, energy prices would soar. But that doesn't faze Obama; if anything, it plays into his whole "green economy" scheme (i.e., throw trillions of dollars against the wall and see if anything sticks).

A federal judge struck down the moratorium, calling the arguments misleading, sloppy, and factually inaccurate. The administration appealed the decision, and lost that too. Undaunted, the president sought a way around the rulings. What happened to respect for the rule of law?

Why is Obama so adamant about imposing a drilling moratorium? Does he plan to use the disaster to nationalize the oil companies? He's already nationalized large sectors of the economy. Could oil be next? Control the nation's energy supply, and you control the lifeblood of the economy.

THE PRESIDENT TRIED TO USE the Gulf disaster to resurrect his stalled environmental legislation. Well before the leak, Obama's agenda included action to address Hollywood's favorite cause célèbre: global warming.

The administration's signature proposal is known as "cap-and-trade" (alternately referred to as "carbon offsets," "emissions trading," or "cap-and-tax"). The legislation would *cap* the amount of carbon an energy producer may emit; to exceed that allotted amount, the "polluter" may purchase, or *trade*, for additional carbon permits. That's a fancy way of describing an enormous energy tax.

Early in 2008, then-Senator Obama brazenly admitted as much to the *San Francisco Chronicle*. The following is an exact quote: "Under my plan of a cap-and-trade system, electricity rates would necessarily skyrocket. Coal-powered plants, you know, natural gas, you name it, whatever the plants were, whatever the industry was, they would have to retrofit their operations. That will cost money. They will pass that money on to consumers."

The *Wall Street Journal* described cap-and-trade as the biggest tax in American history. That contradicts the president's long-forgotten promise not to raise taxes on 95 percent of American families (did anyone actually believe him?). The plan would cost the average household anywhere from $700 to $3,000 in higher energy prices annually. Low-income families would pay the highest percentage of price hikes relative to their income. Business and industry would be forced to slash jobs and increase prices.

Defenders argue that higher energy costs aren't technically a tax, so the president is keeping his word. You be the judge.

Under Obama's cap-and-trade scheme, the United States would lose still more ground to emerging economic powerhouses like China and India, whose governments impose no such environmental hardships on business. Blue-collar jobs and coal-producing regions would be hit disproportionately hard (Obama harbors a virulent distaste for coal, as well as nuclear power, which is the cleanest energy of all, ironically). At least Al Gore and wealthy Hollywood types can sleep easy. They might have to pay a little more to fuel up their private jets, but their lifestyles won't be crimped.

Cap-and-trade cleared the House in 2009 on a vote of 219-212, the same margin by which ObamaCare passed. "This is the biggest job-killing bill that's ever been on the floor of the House of Representatives," argued Minority Leader John Boehner.

The Senate never acted on the legislation, sparing the nation further economic distress (thank goodness for the filibuster). In the midst of a protracted recession, the American people want their leaders to focus on the economy. At a minimum, they don't want Congress jeopardizing even more private-sector jobs.

In the aftermath of the Gulf catastrophe, the administration circulated a memo suggesting that a lame-duck Congress take up cap-and-trade after the midterm elections, when defeated incumbents won't have the voters to worry about. It's increasingly clear that this president is drunk on his own power.

IF CAP-AND-TRADE AMOUNTS to economic suicide, shouldn't Congress, at a bare minimum, be certain that global warming is a truly urgent threat?

The sun is responsible for 98 percent of Earth's warmth, so man's impact on global temperatures is minimal. Solar activity is cyclical. From roughly 1945-1977, the planet experienced a period of global cooling. Temperatures cooled to such an extent that scientists issued dire warnings about the dawn of a new ice age.

Then, temperatures started rising again. This time, scientists told us that global warming threatened the very survival of mankind. Global temperatures reached a peak in 1998 under the influence of El Niño, and then leveled off for eight years. By 2007, Earth entered a new cooling phase. The winters of 2008-2010 were among the coldest and harshest in memory. Yet the global warming meme persisted. Environmental extremists made us feel guilty for driving our cars and heating our homes.

The global warming movement was further discredited by the "Climategate" scandal, which revealed that leading scientists around the world have been playing around with the facts. They had a powerful incentive for doing so: billions have been squandered in taxpayer-financed boondoggles over the years. Global warming is big business for scientists, savvy entrepreneurs, shady filmmakers, and other assorted hucksters. Follow the money: Obama's entire green economy pitch is predicated upon this charade.

It isn't about the environment anymore; what else to explain the president's dispassion toward an ecological disaster occurring in the Gulf on his watch? Like health care, global warming is central to the far-left's socialist utopia. It's yet another way for the federal government to control its subjects.

Amidst concerns over the economy, global warming has lost much of its sizzle as a hot-button political issue. A Pew Research Center poll in 2009 revealed a fourteen-point drop in just one year in the number of Americans who believe global warming is happening, is man-caused, and is a serious problem. According to Rasmussen, 48 percent of voters believe global warming is caused primarily by planetary trends, whereas only 33 percent attribute it mainly to human activity. After back-to-back brutal winters, Europeans started losing their fear of climate change as well.

Note that global warming has been re-branded "climate change." If one title isn't working, just repackage it under a different label, so the theory goes.

LATE IN 2009, PRESIDENT Obama flew to Copenhagen, Denmark for the U.N. Climate Change Conference. The purpose of the trip was to hash out an international climate treaty (which usually implies a transfer of wealth from industrialized nations to developing ones). Throughout the conference, Copenhagen was socked by a blizzard that blanketed much of the northern hemisphere. The irony was rich: Europe was in the midst of its coldest winter in twenty years, yet there stood Obama, pledging to fight global warming at the expense of American jobs.

The conference was the president's second forgettable excursion to Copenhagen. Two months earlier, he swooped into town to persuade the International Olympic Committee to award the 2016 games to Chicago. Obama expected to parlay his popularity abroad into a public relations coup. No doubt, the president had visions of carrying the Olympic torch into his adopted hometown in a glorious, triumphant conclusion to two wildly successful terms as president.

Except that he was told no. The games were awarded to Rio de Janeiro.

To avoid being inconvenienced, the president and first lady flew separately on their mission to Copenhagen. Let the plebeians worry about protecting the environment; the Obamas had urgent business to attend to! The trip cost taxpayers millions and accomplished nothing. But as a consolation, we were kept apprised of Michelle Obama's fashion choices while out on the town.

And for the record, Mrs. Obama called the trip—taken on a private jet with Oprah Winfrey, complete with luxury accommodations, opera, world-class chefs, and an audience with the queen of Denmark—a "sacrifice." Isn't it reassuring to know that such dedicated public servants are willing to suffer for the common good?

CHAPTER 24

A PRESIDENT'S JUDICIAL APPOINTMENTS ensure that his legacy endures well beyond his tenure in office. Cabinet secretaries come and go, but members of the judiciary serve for a lifetime. That's not to say this president hasn't altered history in other ways: his deficit spending is burying our children in debt, he's eroded our international standing, and he's taken over large swaths of the private sector. But Obama's most lasting and dangerous legacy, when all the dust has settled, will be on the federal courts.

Supreme Court appointments are for life. Thus, enormous power is entrusted to a handful of unelected, unaccountable men and women. Obama had an opportunity to make an early appointment to the Supreme Court when Justice David Souter announced his resignation early in 2009. Don't think the timing was a coincidence. Souter and other liberal justices had been biding their time, waiting out Bush's second term, hoping a like-minded president would select their successors.

Souter is prima facie evidence of an out-of-control federal judiciary. Plucked from obscurity in New Hampshire by the elder President Bush,

Souter was touted as a leading conservative legal scholar. Never mind that he was neither conservative nor a scholar; the nation was saddled with his brand of left-wing judicial activism for nearly two decades.

The activism of today's courts—making laws, rather than interpreting them—runs counter to the intentions of the Founding Fathers. As Exhibit A, every time gay marriage has been on the ballot, even in liberal states, the people have voted against it. Homosexual marriage has been sanctioned *only* when unelected judges have imposed it on the people. This happened most recently in California, where one federal judge (who happens to be homosexual himself) nullified the votes of seven million people and declared gay marriage to be a constitutional right.

For decades, liberal judges have legislated from the bench without regard to public opinion. Today, the judiciary is as close to a dictatorship as exists in the United States. It is precisely for this reason that the Framers of the Constitution never intended for the judicial branch to wield such power.

Conservative Justice Antonin Scalia has asked law school audiences, "What is the meaning of the Constitution?" Students give it their best shots, but they never anticipate Scalia's answer: on any given day, the Constitution means whatever five members of the Supreme Court say it means.

OBAMA HAS A RARE OPPORTUNITY to shape the federal judiciary for decades. In just one term, he could make as many as four appointments to the nine-member Supreme Court, an average of one per year (by comparison, Bush and Clinton each made only two appointments in two terms). If Obama is re-elected, he will almost certainly have nominated a majority of justices to the Supreme Court. That's an eerie thought: as many as five or six Obama appointees legislating from the bench for a generation. That type of damage could never be undone.

Obama claimed that he wanted judges who could bring "empathy" (which is code for judicial activism) to the bench. But empathy is in the eye of the beholder. His first nominee to the high court, Sonia Sotomayor, didn't display any of it in the case of *Ricci v. DeStefano*.

In 2006, Frank Ricci and seventeen other white firefighters, along with one Hispanic, sued the city of New Haven, Connecticut when they were denied promotions because of the color of their skin. Though the white firefighters scored higher on the qualifying test than minority applicants, the results were thrown out by New Haven's civil service board. Ricci, who was dyslexic, gave up a second job and spent three months preparing for the exam. His efforts were for naught; Sotomayor, then a federal appeals court judge, sided with the city. Under the Obama/ Sotomayor judicial regime, "empathy" doesn't extend to white males. (This case has a happy ending: on appeal, the Supreme Court sided with Ricci on a 5-4 ruling.)

Sotomayor, who is of Puerto Rican descent, made no bones about her activism. "I would hope that a wise Latina woman with the richness of her experiences would more often than not reach a better conclusion than a white male who hasn't lived that life," she said before several audiences.

Some viewed the statement as racist. While there may have been a grain of truth to the charge, Sotomayor was really telegraphing her own brand of judicial activism. This is unfortunate; the underlying precept of blind justice is that issues of race and gender ought never to influence an impartial judge. The statement revealed more than anything else Sotomayor said during four days of testimony before the Senate Judiciary Committee.

Originalists like Scalia defer to the elected legislative branch; activists like Sotomayor would force their will on the American people. That Obama's first nominee would settle comfortably into the high court's liberal wing was a foregone conclusion.

This president got his second chance in two years to alter the composition of the Supreme Court when longtime liberal stalwart John Paul Stevens announced his retirement. Stevens was another example of a Republican nominee who "evolved" leftward after his confirmation.

Dating to Eisenhower, Republican presidents have named the majority of justices—yet thanks to Stevens, Souter, and other fatuous appointees, the Supreme Court has remained a cauldron of judicial activism. Like Souter, Stevens postponed his resignation until a Democrat occupied the Oval Office. So much for impartiality on the high court.

Upon his announcement, Stevens was praised as the leader of the Court's liberal bloc. "Commitment to expanding freedom," "brave and honorable," and "a record of excellence and integrity" ran the comments. Allow me to dissent. Stevens' body of work can be epitomized by two recent cases in which he sided with government against individual liberties.

In 2008, the Court affirmed, in a too-close-for-comfort 5-4 ruling, our right to keep and bear arms in the case of *District of Columbia v. Heller*. Stevens wrote the minority opinion, arguing that a right clearly enumerated in the Constitution no longer exists. Should Obama replace just one of those five majority justices, the Supreme Court could effectively nullify the Second Amendment. It could happen: Justices Scalia and Anthony Kennedy are in their mid-seventies.

Another example of judicial activism during Stevens' tenure was the infamous *Kelo v. City of New London* decision in 2005. This time, Stevens authored the opinion for the Court's 5-4 majority. Local governments, he wrote, have the right to seize citizens' homes—not to build schools or highways, but to turn the property over to private investors for redevelopment.

Stevens' rulings on these and a range of controversial cases show an appalling disregard for constitutional rights. When liberals champion a cause which wouldn't have a chance of passing the elected legislative branch—that is, when public opinion isn't on their side, which is most of the time—they turn to unelected judges to circumvent the will of the people. Stevens was a willing accomplice to such activism during his thirty-five years on the bench.

Obama's election guaranteed that the ninety-year-old Stevens would be replaced by a successor every bit as activist. Sure enough, the president nominated Ivy League elitist Elena Kagan, who is forty years Stevens' junior. As dean of Harvard Law School, Kagan banned military recruiters on campus as a protest against the armed forces' prohibition on openly gay members. As a Clinton political operative—she has no judicial background—Kagan once compared the National Rifle Association to the KKK. Her appointment didn't alter the ideological composition of the Supreme Court (four liberals, four conservatives, and one centrist), but it effectively preserves that liberal seat for decades to come.

Obama is stocking the federal courts at all levels with judges and justices in his own philosophical image. Even if the voters fire him at the next election, his impact on the judiciary will endure. That's a painful lesson for disgruntled conservatives who stayed home in 2008.

EVEN SOTOMAYOR HAD TO BE stunned to witness the president dressing down the Supreme Court at her first State of the Union. At issue was a recent high court ruling on campaign finance law.

This was the adolescent who never grew up, lashing out at the justices before a national audience: "Last week, the Supreme Court reversed a century of law to open the floodgates for special interests, including foreign corporations, to spend without limit in our elections. Well, I don't think American elections should be bankrolled by America's most powerful interests, or, worse, by foreign entities."

The scolding of the justices to their faces was a major breach of protocol. Like a spoiled child with the stage to himself, Obama used the occasion to throw a tantrum in front of forty-eight million viewers. Democratic members of Congress roared their approval, adding to the inappropriateness of the moment. (By tradition, Supreme Court justices who choose to attend State of the Union addresses make no open displays of emotion.)

Obama was carping about the landmark *Citizens United v. Federal Election Commission* ruling in which the Court upheld, by that familiar 5-4 margin, the First Amendment to the Constitution. Obama, in his customary antibusiness fashion, came down on the side of restricting the political activities of corporations within sixty days of an election.

Six weeks later, Chief Justice John Roberts responded to the president's outburst: "The image of having the members of one branch of government standing up, literally surrounding the Supreme Court, cheering and hollering while the Court, according to the requirements of protocol, has to sit there expressionless, I think is very troubling."

Roberts hinted that the justices may stop attending State of the Union addresses. "I'm not sure why we're there," he added. With that, Obama may have ended an age-old Capitol tradition, the coming together of the three branches of government for one ceremonial evening.

After a year in office, Obama had abandoned any pretense of presidential decorum. The man once billed as postpartisan was now derided as post-American.

SPEAKING OF "FOREIGN ENTITIES" bankrolling American elections, to quote the president, we still have no idea where all of his campaign cash came from. The Obama money machine raised such an obscene amount that the candidate reneged on his commitment to abide by public financing limitations. (This was one of the great underreported stories of the election. The press corps would have guillotined Bush or McCain, had they violated a similar pledge. Obama was given a pass.)

To date, more than $200 million raised by the Obama campaign has never been sourced. That's a gap the size of the Grand Canyon.

Obama boasted about utilizing the Internet as a means of fundraising. Indeed, the web has made it easier for individuals to contribute money—and commit fraud. A single donor can send money under different aliases, or foreigners can contribute from abroad. (Candidates are prohibited from accepting contributions from noncitizens.)

Per federal campaign law, donors who contribute $200 or less need not be identified. In the spirit of full disclosure, the McCain campaign released the names of all its donors, large and small. The Obama campaign declined to do likewise. McCain went so far as to require proof of U.S. citizenship before accepting any overseas contributions. The Obama camp did not ask for such proof until late in the election cycle, by which time it had raised more money (a record-shattering $650 million) than it could possibly spend.

Libyan dictator Moammar Khadafi openly boasted that Muslims throughout the Middle East were contributing to Obama. A series of fundraisers were held in Nigeria, collecting an estimated $900,000 for the Democratic nominee. The Obama campaign site accepted money via untraceable, prepaid credit cards, opening the floodgates to millions of dollars in illegal contributions. We'll never know the whole story. That the campaign brazenly flouted the law is beyond dispute.

We'll also never know what role international financiers, such as the rabidly anti-American George Soros, played in Obama's fundraising. What we do know is that foreign entities, many of which don't have the United States' best interest at heart, attempted to influence the outcome of our election. They have to be happy with the results.

CHAPTER 25

HALF A MILLION ILLEGAL IMMIGRANTS call Arizona home, a fivefold increase since 1990. During those two decades, a crime wave has swept the state. Phoenix is now the kidnapping capital of the United States. Many parts of Arizona are unsafe and uninhabitable, owing to human smuggling, drug trafficking, and imported poverty.

The state has spent $750 million on prison costs for illegal immigrant offenders since 2003. Arizona's schools, hospitals, and social services are stretched beyond their limits. The situation has become economically unsustainable for the state's taxpayers. That is not hard-hearted or racist; it is reality.

The federal government refused to act. The people of Arizona did.

Senate Bill 1070, the Support Our Law Enforcement and Safe Neighborhoods Act, makes it a misdemeanor to be an alien in the state of Arizona without proper documentation as required by federal immigration law. In other words, SB 1070 authorizes state and local law enforcement agencies to enforce statutes which are already on the books. A no-brainer.

The law enjoys widespread popular support. A Rasmussen poll showed 70 percent of Arizonans back the measure. Nationally, the numbers are similar: by a three-to-one margin, Americans believe a police officer should check the immigration status of anyone stopped for a traffic violation, if he or she suspects the individual is in the country illegally. That's the heart of the Arizona law.

The measure sparked a flurry of protests from the usual left-wing suspects. Interest groups organized rallies, marches, and boycotts, and even recruited harebrained celebrities like Shakira and Lady Gaga to speak out against the law. But it's important to remember that these protesters represent a minority of the populace. These are Alinsky tactics: like pufferfish, professional organizers know how to exaggerate their size and grab the headlines.

Only individuals with a direct economic, familial, or political stake in illegal immigration could realistically oppose the law. One of those is the president.

In knee-jerk fashion, Obama, Holder, and Napolitano came out against SB 1070, before they'd even had a chance to read it. Obama contended that immigration enforcement is a federal responsibility. He must take us for a nation of fools: administrations of both parties have lacked the political will to enforce the borders for at least twenty years. That's what finally compelled Arizona to take action. Ironically, it was Napolitano, as governor of Arizona in 2005, who declared a state of emergency along the southwest border.

The law explicitly prohibits any form of racial or ethnic profiling, another concern professed by administration officials.

Ignoring the will of the majority of Arizonans, Obama's Justice Department sued the state to block implementation of the law. Once again, the people lost. A left-wing federal judge voided key provisions of the statute in July 2010.

In one high-profile ruling after another, federal judges have effectively nullified the Tenth Amendment to the Constitution, the principle of states' rights.

The legal victory played into Obama's larger ideological objectives. Long a supporter of open borders, the president views illegal immigration as a means of transforming the nation demographically, economically, and politically. He even suggested using the controversy—never let a crisis go to waste!—to revisit comprehensive immigration reform at the federal level. To clarify, "comprehensive" reform means "amnesty" or a "path to citizenship" for illegal immigrants.

If every survey is to be believed, Americans overwhelmingly object to amnesty for lawbreakers. First and foremost, they want the borders secured. Yet the Washington elites think they know better.

Republicans are far from blameless on the issue. Bush and McCain previously pushed comprehensive reform; the McCain-Kennedy bill would have become law in 2007 if not for a furious wave of opposition rallied by talk radio. Bush was on board as a sop to business groups, who wanted a cheap source of labor (also, his "compassionate conservatism" sometimes meant thinking with his heart instead of his head).

Obama's motives are different. He couldn't care less about the needs of business, and his heart isn't nearly the size of Bush's. Obama sees power. In his view, amnesty would enfranchise millions of new Democratic voters, bringing about a permanent governing majority. His goal is to establish an enduring socialist state—à la Europe—in which the lower class trades its votes for benefits. To Obama, illegal immigration is a means to a political and economic end.

The irony is that most immigrants should be a natural fit for the Republican Party. Most believe profoundly in growth and opportunity. Many have risked their lives to enjoy our great freedoms. The last thing they want is to swap one corrupt, socialist hellhole for another.

The longer immigrants are integrated into American society, and the older they get, the more they tend to vote Republican. According to a survey by the Latino Coalition, more Hispanic voters consider themselves conservative than liberal.

Republicans have to do a better job of promoting themselves to this important and fast-growing constituency. Democrats have it easy: they can just promise money for nothing. Republicans need to be more creative. Florida's Rubio suggests the GOP market itself as the pro-*legal* immigration party. That's sage advice.

AFTER THE ELECTION, Andy Stern, then-president of the 2.2 million-member SEIU, informed Obama that the union was "demanding payback" on its investment. The SEIU was one of Obama's earliest and most visible backers, raising funds and actively campaigning for him since his days as a state senator. By some estimates, it pumped $30 million into the Obama presidential campaign. Now, declared its longtime president, it was payback time.

And did the union ever cash in on its investment, beginning with passage of its top two priorities, the stimulus bill and ObamaCare. Next on the SEIU's shopping list is the Employee Free Choice Act, or "card check." The name is intentionally deceiving; the act has nothing to do with offering additional choices to workers. Just the opposite: the measure would actually coerce employees into unionizing.

Under today's laws, if workers in the United States wish to unionize, they cast votes via secret ballot; that's a time-honored tradition. The problem for big labor is that more private-sector employees have been choosing not to organize in recent years, and union membership has plummeted. That scenario is bad for union bosses and Democrats alike.

Card check legislation would do away with the secret ballot. Employees would instead be required to sign unionization cards in the presence of organizers and co-workers. Should the majority of employees sign up, the entire shop would be unionized. The pressure would be enormous. Failure to sign could subject an individual to untold harassment and retribution.

Such a scenario would fulfill one of Obama's political goals: union membership would soar, and those dues would make their way into the coffers of friendly (Democratic) candidates. Card check would also increase government control over private industry—a running theme of the Obama presidency—by mandating federal arbitration between employers and unions. Care to guess which side Obama's Department of Labor would come down on?

Mass unionization would impose yet another hardship on the beleaguered private sector. Card check hasn't passed yet, but Obama won't give up pushing for it.

Stern also enjoyed payback on a personal level when the president named him to the National Commission on Fiscal Responsibility and Reform (a.k.a. the deficit panel). Obama's appointment of the pro-labor radical was denounced by Republicans and business groups. *Investor's Business Daily* likened it to "having a serial arsonist organize Fire Prevention Week."

Stern is permitted to serve on the panel only because he is not a lobbyist; at least, not technically. The longtime SEIU chief has carried on all the duties of a lobbyist and is one of the most active influence peddlers in the Obama White House, yet he never registered as a lobbyist, in possible violation of federal law.

OBAMA'S RELATIONSHIP WITH LOBBYISTS is complicated. Before the election, the candidate struck a populist note. To hear him put it, the lobbying profession ranked somewhere between mass murder and harlotry. His promise that lobbyists "won't find a job in my White House" was a tried-and-true applause line on the campaign trail.

A week after the election, he was hiring lobbyists. Like crazy.

As many as forty former lobbyists hold senior positions in the administration, including Obama's CIA director and three cabinet secretaries. Former lobbyists for Raytheon and Goldman Sachs now hold top positions at the Pentagon and Treasury Department, respectively.

Ever in campaign mode, Obama reiterated his long-abandoned pledge during his 2010 State of the Union address. "We've excluded lobbyists from policymaking jobs," he proclaimed in a moment of barefaced effrontery. White House advisers scrambled to square the discrepancy. It just depends on your definitions of lobbyist and policymaking! If imitation is the sincerest form of flattery, Bill Clinton is bursting with pride.

It wasn't Obama's first about-face on the issue of lobbying. Soon after he arrived in the Senate, Obama pledged to work with McCain on a bipartisan lobbyist disclosure package. Democratic leaders, eager to use ethics as a sledgehammer against the Republican Congress, warned Obama not to play nice. The spineless freshman promptly welched on his commitment to work with McCain.

Bad move. The old pilot delivered the smackdown on the young hotshot. "I concluded your professed concern for...the public interest was genuine and admirable. Thank you for disabusing me of such notions," wrote McCain.

Would that he'd shown some of that spark during the election!

DEMOCRATS GAINED CONTROL OF both houses of Congress in January 2007. By coincidence or not, the recession officially began eleven months later. While there was no shortage of blame, two veteran lawmakers, Senator Christopher Dodd and Representative Barney Frank, who respectively chair the Senate and House Banking Committees, had their handprints all over the crisis. It is ironic then that Dodd and Frank led the president's "reform" of the financial services industry.

Their goals, ostensibly, were to end taxpayer bailouts and to minimize the possibility of future financial meltdowns. To give an air of populism to the proceedings, Obama traveled to New York to mete out a scolding to Wall Street bigwigs. But the president doth protest too much. Large Wall Street firms, including Goldman Sachs and Citibank, two recipients of bailout money, came out in support of the administration's so-called reforms. That's like a seventh-grader favoring stricter detention policy. Republicans smelled a rat.

(Contrary to popular belief, Wall Street contributes more to Democratic candidates. Goldman Sachs, which has since been charged with fraud, gave three times as much to Democrats than Republicans in the 2008 election cycle. Small businesses on the other hand, which have neither asked for nor received a bailout, remain staunchly Republican.)

Under the Dodd-Frank plan, larger firms, many of which were at the heart of the original financial crisis, will survive, and even thrive. The most burdensome regulations fall on smaller institutions and local community banks. That could drive them out of business, or allow the big boys to acquire them. The reforms also grant federal regulators sweeping new powers to break up or seize financial firms, which is a frightening scenario in itself.

The legislation mandates that financial institutions observe race and gender quotas, but does nothing to reform Fannie Mae or Freddie Mac. In the first quarter of 2010 alone, Fannie and Freddie reported multibillion dollar losses. They requested another $20 billion from Congress, in addition to the nearly $145 billion the agencies have already received from taxpayers. Republican senators introduced an amendment to address these out-of-control money pits. In the Democratic-controlled Senate, it went nowhere.

The Dodd-Frank plan contains a $50 billion "orderly resolution fund"—a permanent bailout fund for the Democrats' Wall Street allies. (Populist rhetoric notwithstanding, Obama has never met a bailout he didn't like.) It makes the tools of TARP permanent, thereby rewarding the "too-big-to-fail" institutions. In other words, taxpayers will continue to subsidize Wall Street's risky behavior.

The Wall Street Reform and Consumer Protection Act of 2010, a.k.a. financial reform, is little more than a vehicle for Obama and the Democrats to reward politically-connected fat cats, while again expanding the power of government over the little guy. Whether or not by design, the measure fails to address the root causes of the original financial crisis.

Democrats ignored minority Republicans throughout the deliberations, and then assailed them for not joining their cabal. The legislation passed after Senate leaders snagged the votes of three New England Republicans (Snowe, Collins, and surprisingly, Brown). For the umpteenth time, a sweeping Obama initiative eked through Congress on a nearly party-line vote.

CHAPTER 26

IF WORDS ARE TO BE believed, Michelle Obama is her husband's ideological soulmate. At an early campaign stop in Wisconsin, where Barack was performing better than expected in the polls, Mrs. Obama made the mistake of going off-script and speaking her heart:

"For the first time in my adult lifetime, I'm really proud of my country."

A slip of the tongue? Taken out of context? Maybe…except she repeated the comment verbatim at her next appearance, before campaign officials hastily intervened. It was a rare moment of candor for someone so immersed in the world of politics.

Michelle and Barack Obama believe the United States is a fundamentally flawed nation; one in need of a radical makeover. The candidate parlayed this conviction into his amorphous yet successful campaign slogan, "Change You Can Believe In."

The media told us Obama was postracial. That narrative was deflated with a deafening *pop!* when he was asked about the racially charged arrest of Professor Henry Louis Gates Jr. by the Cambridge

Police Department. The appropriate answer would have been: "That's an ongoing investigation, and I don't have all the facts. Besides, the president has responsibilities far greater than butting in on a local police matter, so I'm going to keep my mouth shut for once in my life."

But, no. Obama couldn't resist the temptation to interject himself directly into the controversy. The Cambridge police had acted "stupidly," opined the president.

To almost no one's surprise, Obama's impromptu assessment of the incident was wrong. Professor Gates was the one who'd acted belligerently, screaming at Sgt. James Crowley—a respected officer with a sterling reputation, it turned out. But this president can never admit a mistake, nor can he shy away from the cameras and microphones. Ever.

In an effort at damage control, Obama invited Gates and Crowley to join him and Biden for a beer (that's how regular guys bond, right?). The much-hyped "beer summit"—four ill-at-ease men sitting around an oversized table, in full view of the cameras—was indeed a lesson for the nation: we learned there was only one man at that table you'd want in a foxhole with you. At least it wasn't a total waste.

CONSERVATIVE TALK RADIO finds itself atop the Democrats' enemies list. Obama would love to silence his critics permanently, if only he could. The president's men dusted off the archaic (and inaptly named) Fairness Doctrine as a government-sanctioned means of censorship.

Liberal talk radio has failed nearly everywhere. It's never been able to match the success of conservative talk, with its towering personalities: Limbaugh, Hannity, Savage, Beck, et al. Air America, home of those learned scholars Al Franken and Janeane Garofalo, famously tanked after five years of miserable ratings. Even at the local level, conservative programming enjoys near-universal dominance over its liberal counterparts.

This mystery has long confounded the left. Let's demystify it for them.

Liberals dominate nearly every means of mass communication in this country: the media, Hollywood, and academia. Young minds are brainwashed by radical teachers and professors on a daily basis. We can hardly enjoy television or a movie anymore without enduring an anti-family, antimilitary, anticapitalism screed. All considered, it's a wonder that conservative Republicans can get elected anywhere in the country. The playing field is uneven, and the referees are pulling for the other side.

The mainstream news media are largely responsible for their own demise. It's fashionable to blame the Internet, but that's only part of it. Patriotic Americans, fed up with the smarmy, left-wing bias of their daily newspapers, have voted with their feet. No one wants to pay to have his or her values belittled. As a result, many dailies aren't profitable anymore. Likewise, network news ratings are at an all-time low.

While liberals are satisfied with what they're getting from the mainstream media, conservatives have been forced to look elsewhere for news and information. Since the debut of Rush Limbaugh, talk radio has filled that vacuum. Rather than celebrate dissent, however, Obama and his minions want to stifle it. In the Fairness Doctrine, a 1940s-era relic that was jettisoned by Congress in 1987, Democrats sought a roundabout means of doing so.

If passed, the doctrine would compel stations to grant equal time to conservative and liberal programming. At a minimum, such a requirement would cut the airtime of conservative talk in half. But that's only the beginning. For many radio stations, the anemic ratings of their newly-mandated liberal programming would wipe them out financially. Smaller stations are especially vulnerable: they'd be forced to drop all political talk—or close their doors entirely.

Obama is smart enough to realize that even if the Fairness Doctrine passed Congress, it would be struck down by the courts faster than you can say "unconstitutional." So White House lawyers devised a backdoor means of achieving the same ends. One method could come in the form of "diversity" (or "localism"), which would authorize the Federal Communications Commission (FCC) to promote "diversity of ownership of stations" and require station owners to "operate in the public interest."

Of course, the interpretations of diversity and public interest would be left to the FCC, which is controlled by Democrats. Broadcasters would be forced to play ball with federal bureaucrats, lest their licenses be held hostage. Such a cloak-and-dagger plot to subdue free speech is every bit as dangerous as overt legislative action. When elected officials use the powers of government to silence their critics, that's censorship. And censorship is a stone's throw away from dictatorship.

THE INTERNATIONAL DELIRIUM surrounding Obama's celebrity reached a crescendo with the announcement that he'd been awarded the 2009 Nobel Peace Prize. It was the first time the prize was awarded to an individual for doing...nothing.

Officially, Obama won for his rhetoric. Unofficially, he won for being the un-Bush. The heretofore distinguished Nobel Committee, comprised of five Norwegian leftists, lost much of its credibility. That a once-prestigious award has been downgraded to a cheap political statement is regrettable. What's next, a Nobel Prize in Happy Meals?

Obama flew to Oslo, gave his Nobel lecture and then, to the dismay of the Norwegian people, skipped out on a round of events traditionally attended by the prizewinner. He thus managed the impossible: winning an award for doing nothing, and then offending the country that awarded it.

Obama's trophy case must be getting crowded. He's also won two Grammy Awards. In 2006, he was awarded a Grammy for reading the audio version of his memoir, *Dreams from My Father*, though it'd been published in book form nine years earlier. He won a second Grammy Award in 2008 for reading *The Audacity of Hope*, its Rev. Wright-inspired sequel.

The two books were combined into one audio CD entitled—this is serious—*The Essential Barack Obama*. The CD goes for about $33 on Amazon. Some people just can't get enough of the man's voice. Personally, I'd rather have a root canal.

OBAMA'S RHETORIC HAS OFTEN bordered on the megalomaniacal: "A beam of light will come down upon you, you will experience an epiphany, and you will suddenly realize that you must go to the polls and vote for Obama." He also declared that his election was "the moment when the rise of the oceans began to slow, and our planet began to heal." While some of us laughed, millions of our countrymen lapped up his words like manna from heaven.

In Obama's world, everything is about him. Since bursting onto the national scene, he's become addicted to the word "unprecedented." According to the president, all things Obama—his crowds, speeches, fundraising, Internet presence, and historic candidacy—are unprecedented.

The Obama campaign was unprecedented in another way: it was the first time in which a candidate's full name was off-limits. Any mention of his middle name, Hussein, was deemed mean-spirited and racist. Even McCain rushed to apologize when one of his supporters made reference to Obama's full name.

The origin of the name Hussein is Arabic; it means "good" or "handsome." It was, of course, his father's middle name, and then his.

Throughout the campaign, the media went to great lengths to celebrate Obama's biography—his multicultural background, his unique childhood experiences, his family's connections to three continents, and so on. Yet the candidate bristled at any mention of his middle name, at least until after the election. The flap over the name revealed Obama's distinctively thin skin. That particular character defect is far more bothersome than a name.

The presidency is so much more than just giving speeches, which is all Obama had done prior to his inauguration. It is the hardest job in human history. Every problem in the world ends up in your in-box. Criticism is as automatic as the rising sun.

Obama's peevishness was evident during a testy meeting with the Senate Republican caucus. "He needs to take a Valium before he comes in and talks to Republicans. He's pretty thin-skinned," noted Senator Pat Roberts of Kansas.

In the heat of the 2010 midterm elections, with polls showing a massive backlash against the Democrats' ideological overreach, Obama cracked. "They talk about me like a dog!" he complained of political opponents. Such grousing might be expected of an insecure preteen, but not the most powerful man on earth.

Two years into Obama's presidency, with the pressures mounting, it was increasingly clear that this community organizer is not up to the job. The indications were there before the election. We ignore them again at our peril.

CHAPTER 27

B ARACK OBAMA HAS MASTERED the Machiavellian ability to say one thing but do the opposite.

He promised hope, and then brought the Chicago political machine to Washington.

He promised change, and then stocked the White House with lobbyists and Clinton retreads.

He promised bipartisanship, and then rammed through his major policy initiatives on party-line votes.

Obama opposes educational choice, yet he sends his daughters to an expensive private school.

He vowed to run "the most transparent administration in history," but drafted his most important legislation out of the public view. He also appointed dozens of czars to run large swaths of the federal bureaucracy with no oversight or accountability.

He pilloried President Bush for making recess appointments (bypassing Senate confirmation), but has made sixteen of his own.

Most notably, he tapped Dr. Donald Berwick, a proponent of health care rationing, to run the nation's Medicare and Medicaid programs.

Obama claims he opposes gay marriage, while coming out against California's Proposition 8, which defined marriage as being between a man and a woman. He's also opposed to the Defense of Marriage Act.

He promised openness, and then went more than three hundred days without holding a press conference. (The longest Bush went was 214 days—and opponents blasted him for secrecy.)

His campaign played up his educational bona fides, yet he has refused to release his college records.

Obama is fond of saying "words matter," but has little use for symbols. Notably, he refused to wear an American flag lapel pin for much of the campaign.

As a candidate, he campaigned aggressively for Nevada's electoral votes, and then twice warned businesses not to travel to Las Vegas. That remains a sore point with Vegas locals; the Democratic mayor declared that Obama is no longer welcome in his city.

A stickler for political correctness, Obama mocked the Special Olympics on *The Tonight Show*.

In his first State of the Union, the former constitutional law instructor attributed a line from the Declaration of Independence to the Constitution.

In Europe, he made reference to the Austrian language, which doesn't exist.

He mispronounced navy corpsman as "corpse-man" three times. (Imagine if Bush had done that!)

After describing Ground Zero as "hallowed ground," he came out in support of a victory mosque to be built near the site of the former World Trade Center.

His administration found time to sue Arizona over its popular immigration law, while dismissing charges against members of the New

Black Panther Party, who were videotaped intimidating voters on the day of Obama's election.

He railed against Wall Street and Big Oil, while raking in millions in contributions from them. The Obama money machine was the largest recipient of campaign funds from BP over the past twenty years.

He bragged that the stimulus would fund thousands of "shovel-ready" construction and infrastructure projects across the nation. By late 2010—with the stimulus clearly a failure—he sheepishly admitted, "There's no such thing as shovel-ready projects."

OBAMA MIGHT BE THE first person to have used a teleprompter while speaking in a sixth-grade classroom. Another time, he accidentally read remarks intended for the Irish Prime Minister. The audience laughed when Obama thanked himself for inviting himself to be there.

Early in his presidency, Obama was delivering remarks on urban policy when one of his teleprompters broke loose and crashed to the ground (cue the jokes: the prompter couldn't take it anymore and killed itself). He continued speaking, forced to read off the prompter to his right. His dependence on the gadgets inspired the nickname, teleprompter in chief.

This president reminds you of the schmoozer who blows everyone away during the interview, then ends up being woefully unqualified for the job.

No other president, certainly within recent memory, has roused as many concerns relating to his experience, judgment, ideology, and values, as our current commander in chief. The United States has been blessed with great presidents throughout its history, including Washington, Jefferson, Lincoln, and Reagan, to name a few. We've also endured our share of failures: Buchanan, Grant, Harding, and Carter, among others.

As a student of history, I'm willing to make this prediction with both confidence and sadness: in a century's time, scholars will rank Obama as the worst of the worst.

That's assuming the nation, as we know it, survives his presidency. But take heart; survive we will, and even thrive once more. The great glory of our nation will persevere.

THE ELECTION OF 2008 should be regarded, to use an educator's lexicon, as a teachable moment. We who came of age during a different chapter in history have failed our current generation. Today's youth never lived through the horrors of Nazism and communism. Most have no recollection of our Cold War struggles against a truly evil empire. Few even understand the difference between socialism and capitalism. They have little appreciation for the greatness, the heroism, and the generosity of the United States of America.

This generation doesn't understand what an awesome gift they've been given: the honor and privilege of being an American. Not this "citizen of the world" inanity, but a *United States* citizen.

Rasmussen reports that only 54 percent of Americans now believe the United States is a nation with "liberty and justice for all." Nearly half either disagree with the statement, or are unsure. That's astounding. Perhaps political correctness really has consumed our society. It's the same self-destructive mind-set that shames advertisers from using the word "Christmas" at Christmas.

Recently, one of my middle-schoolers remarked, "I don't see what's so great about this country." I was struck by his nonchalance. The rest of the class never batted an eye. In my day—which wasn't that long ago—only an outcast or a miscreant would have uttered anything so incendiary, and the other kids would've jumped all over him. *Them's fightin' words.*

And then it hit me: today's generation never inherited those values. Somewhere along the line, we forgot to instill in them what it means to be an American.

It's not their fault; they were never taught. *We* failed. That's what made the election of a Barack Obama possible.

To answer my student, I posited the classic Statue of Liberty theorem: the greatness of a nation can be measured by the number of people who want to get out, compared to the number who want to get in. Millions throughout the world are waiting in line to partake of our great freedoms, many risking their lives to do so. By that standard alone, the United States shines like a beacon of hope and opportunity to the huddled masses of the world.

I believe I had a convert.

Historians will note that in the year 2008, the American people were hurt and confused and betrayed and angry. A struggling nation took a gamble on a gifted orator but an untested leader, a manipulator who seized upon a crisis, a demagogue with a hidden agenda.

A man who doesn't share the country's values.

We have an opportunity to change that, if we haven't lost heart. Perhaps the most important virtue of our great republic is the right to correct a mistake at the ballot box. Barack Obama stands for re-election in 2012. Get involved. Help financially. Spread the word. Most of all, pray for your country. This will be the single most important presidential election in American history.

Come January 20, 2013, let's all wake up from this national nightmare.

ABOUT THE AUTHOR

Nelson Anderson has a diverse background with experience in engineering, politics, and education. He earned his graduate degree from the University of San Diego. Nelson loves baseball, football, cooking, reading, working out, and of course, politics.

You can contact the author at ObamaAuthor@ymail.com

ACKNOWLEDGEMENTS

WRITING A BOOK ISN'T EASY. I remember watching a rerun of the "Odd Couple," in which Oscar had two days to complete a fifty-thousand word manuscript. The pressure was getting to him, so Felix took him out to the countryside. Naturally, things only got worse. A funny episode.

Two days? I remember thinking. *A year isn't enough!*

When I'd nearly completed my manuscript, a fellow author asked if I hated it yet. "It's a love-hate relationship," he explained. And I could see his point. There's pressure involved—lots of it—especially when your deadline is near and the publisher is burning up the phone lines. However, I loved every minute of this. *Loved it!* I never even suffered writers' block—but then again, Obama provides plenty of material to keep an author busy.

Granted, I sacrificed two summer vacations (capitalizing on one of the perks of teaching) and untold evenings and weekends to work on this book. Now that it's finished, I can have a social life again. But still,

I enjoyed every moment I spent on this well-worn keyboard. This message and mission are that important to me.

It's astonishing how long it takes to publish a book, and how much is involved behind the scenes. There are the editing, design, and printing phases, not to mention the negotiations with retailers, websites, and distributors. Dinosaurs can go extinct in the time it takes to publish a book. Nevertheless, I am indebted to so many for the success of *OBAMA: Our National Nightmare*:

To my publisher, for your support and patience; to my parents, for their love, and for providing a moral compass all my life; to my sister, who is appreciated more than she knows; to my friends, who've been wondering if I'm still alive; to my students, for making me laugh every day; to Dr. David and Mrs. Linda Mumford, for advice and encouragement; and to my fellow tea partiers, for truly being the salt of the earth. God bless.

www.ingramcontent.com/pod-product-compliance
Lightning Source LLC
Chambersburg PA
CBHW030312290526
45785CB00001B/326